GW00913422

ONE-TO-ONE

Sophie Peace

First published in 2003 by Authentic Lifestyle

09 08 07 06 05 04 03   7 6 5 4 3 2 1

Authentic Lifestyle is an imprint of Authentic Media,
P.O. Box 300, Carlisle, Cumbria, CA3 0QS, UK
and, PO Box 1047, Waynesboro, GA 30830-2047, USA
www.paternoster-publishing.com

British Library Cataloguing in Publication Data
A catalogue record for this book is available from the
British Library

ISBN 1-85078-488-4

Cover Design by Sam Redwood
Printed in Great Britain by Cox and Wyman, Reading

To Peter and Jane Peace,
models of unconditional love
and selfless service

Contents

Acknowledgements xi

Foreword xv

Introduction xvii

1 What is One-to-One Work? 1
Definitions 1
Biblical basis 4
Aims 8
Advantages 15
Study guide 24

2 Getting Involved 26
Who me? 26
Who with? 35
Potential dangers 41
Study guide 50

3 What's Involved? **51**
Prayer 51
Bible study 54
Friendship 65
Study guide 76

4 Meeting Regularly to Study the Bible Before You Meet **77**
Setting up the meetings 77
Bible study preparation 84
Writing the study 89
Study guide 93

5 Meeting Regularly to Study the Bible When You Meet **95**
Practicalities 95
Leading the study 97
Other issues to address 110
Training 115
Study guide 124

6 Meeting Occasionally **126**
Making conversations count 126
Encouragement 133
Rebuke 135
Correction 136
Challenge 138
Bible passages for specific issues 139
Study guide 141

7 Other Considerations **143**
Accountability 143
Pastoral issues 144
Moving on 152
Study guide 156

8 Resources **157**
Study resources 157
Books to read and recommend 173
Other helps – 177
tape ministries, Internet resources
and counselling organizations

Appendix
Growing your Relationship
with God (a note on 'Quiet Times') **181**

Endnotes **188**

Acknowledgements

This book is the fruit of countless people's wisdom and experience gathered through interviews and questionnaires. If it were merely my insights, the book would have been a lot shorter. There are a number of people I want to mention for special thanks. The first is Rico Tice. Without him this book would not have been written. It was because of his vision and passion for one-to-one work that this material ever came to be written down and distributed. Rico, as ever, I thank you for your trust in the sovereignty of God that means you take risks with people and push them out of their comfort zones! I never would have carried on without your constant encouragement, input and inspiration.

Adrian May has put many hours of work into this project. He wrote the 'Bible study' section in chapter 3, contributed much of the material in chapter 6, and put together the study guides you will find at the end of each chapter. Thank you for your humble desire to live out the gospel in so many quiet but significant ways. Andrew Sach also deserves similar thanks. He has edited the material at many different stages with such patience, meticulousness and wisdom. He has also helped with the sample studies of Colossians. Thank you for your invaluable contributions and encouragement, Sachy! To Nigel and Elisa Beynon, who have respectively contributed material and edited the manuscript, my thanks for your time, wisdom and support.

I would also like to thank the following people for their comments on the various drafts of the book: Sam Allberry, Holly Burn, Ralph Cunnington, Ros Furlong, David Jackman, Sydnie Jordan, Elsie Maxwell, Kevin Murdoch, Brian O'Donoghue, Melanie Stone, Amy Stroud, Jeremy Thomas, Helen Willcox and Michael You.

Last but not least are those whom I interviewed about their many years of experience of one-to-one work: Richard Bewes, David and Susie Fletcher, Doug Olsen, Vaughan Roberts, Carrie Sandom, Peter Southwell and John Stott.

There are dozens and dozens of others who have filled in questionnaires and provided material for the 'personal anecdote boxes'. Thank you all for your time in contributing to this book.

Finally, to all those I have met with one-to-one: meeting regularly with each of you has been one of the most encouraging, challenging and rewarding parts of my life so far. Thank you!

Foreword

By the Rev. Rico Tice

If you understand this book and put its principles into practice, then when it comes to Christian service you will never be remotely redundant again. Indeed, you'll be absolute gold dust in any church family. I confess that this book, on working with individuals one-to-one was born out of frustration, as over three years at theological college and then over nine years at All Souls, I saw so many able Christians who were not involved with the work of the church, which is to make disciples (Mt. 28:19). Time and again I found myself internally screaming – if only they knew how to work one-to-one with an individual rather than just sitting there getting resentful that they were not being given any work to do!

By contrast, I found these words from the first commentary I ever read ringing in my ears. Here John Stott comments on the spiritual friendship between Paul and the young Timothy and he compares that relationship to the one he experienced as a young Christian.

> I thank God for the man who led me to Christ and for the extraordinary devotion with which he nurtured me in the early years of my Christian life. He wrote to me every week for, I think, seven years. He also prayed for me every day. I believe he still does. I can only begin to guess what I owe, under God, to such a faithful friend and pastor.[1]

That paragraph opened my eyes to the importance of working with people one-to-one. I was so struck by it that I once showed it to Michael Green at a conference. He read it and said, with no little emotion in his voice, 'The same man worked with me one-to-one.'

If only we could produce individuals who could do this work now. I am just so incredibly grateful to Sophie Peace, who has put in countless hours researching, writing, interviewing and thinking so that we can demystify one-to-one work and give Christian people a methodology to do it. I really think that, having grasped these principles, all we then need to do is pray for a tiny part of the heart Paul had for the Galatians: 'My dear children, for whom I am again in the pains of childbirth until Christ is formed in you' (Gal. 4:19).

The Rev. Rico Tice

Introduction

> Therefore go and make disciples of all nations, baptising them in the name of the Father and of the Son and of the Holy Spirit, and teaching them to obey everything I have commanded you. And surely I am with you always, to the very end of the age.
>
> Matthew 28:19–20

Looking back at the key turning points in your journey of faith – your coming to Christ or maybe big steps forward in your walk with him – odds are there will be certain individuals who have deeply influenced you at these points; individuals who cared and gave you their time, who taught you from the Scriptures and prayed for you.

The gospel is all about changed lives. The kingdom of God advances one person at a time as individuals are born again by God's Spirit and increasingly transformed into the likeness of Christ. While Western culture exalts the individual far above the community, to a place which God never intended, it is still possible for us to miss the significance of the individual in our churches if the teaching and application of God's word is done only corporately.

The evangelical church around the world today might be growing, but there is a danger if that growth is shallow – where there is little depth of understanding and of true discipleship. What is often lacking is a commitment to following the Lord Jesus that thoroughly affects every area of a person's life. Could this be because individuals, specifically, are not being trained to study and apply the Scriptures for themselves and in turn to help others grow in their discipleship?

This book was born out of the conviction that we need many more members of the body of Christ to be exercising a personal ministry of reaching out to individuals outside the church and building up those within the church to make disciples: to be teaching and modelling the gospel, 'one to another'. This is 'one-to-one' work. It is *one Christian taking the initiative with another individual to help them know Christ better and obey him more fully, through studying the scriptures, prayer (for and with them) and sharing one's life with them – and leaving the results to God*. This initiative should, where possible, be taken in the context of accountability to one's immediate

Christian leadership, whether at church, Christian Union or youth camp.

Robert's story

When I first met with someone to read the Bible one to one in 1994, I found it absolutely brilliant. Meeting one to one made me work hard at understanding God's word, which was sometimes tough going, but really rewarding. Whats more, studying the Bible with someone else meant that we got to know each other well and could talk and pray openly and honestly about what God was saying to us. Also, I saw at first hand from my friend what it looks like to put the Bible into practice, which was a real help to me in living as a Christian. Now, eight years on, we're still good friends, and both love meeting up with others to study God's word and pray together.

The aim of this book

So why is this key ministry focusing on individuals happening so little in our churches today? Probably the biggest reasons are the fear of getting it wrong or the fear of looking presumptuous or arrogant for suggesting to someone that they might benefit from meeting up with you. This book aims to counter these fears, and to provide guidelines and help for anyone interested in playing their part in Christ's commission to make disciples.

The biggest question with one-to-one work is usually, 'How?' Because one-to-one work is in its very nature personal and to a certain extent private, it can have a mysterious quality about it for those who have never experienced such a friendship themselves. This book aims to demystify one-to-one or personal work and provide some practical advice on meeting up with a fellow Christian (or non-Christian) to encourage them in their faith. I make no claims to be comprehensive and stress that I have given only general principles that can be adapted to fit individual personalities, gifts and circumstances. It has been difficult to find the balance between being specific enough to be helpful, but general enough not to be restrictive.

Most of the material in this book has been gathered from questionnaires and interviews with those experienced in this type of ministry. There is wisdom gleaned not only from those who have 'led' the one-to-one meetings, but also from those who have been the 'recipients' of such work. They have been questioned on both the positive and negative elements of their experience. Many of these personal anecdotes are contained within 'boxes' throughout the book. I have included them to emphasize the possibility of diversity and flexibility around the principles noted in the text as well as to put some 'flesh on the bones'!

Samantha's story

After a few weeks at my new church in London, an older woman there asked me if I wanted to 'meet regularly to read the Bible' with her. Now I'm not someone from a Christian family and had only been a Christian for four or five months, so this idea was completely alien to me. On leaving church I phoned my boyfriend immediately, asking him what this would involve. He explained that we would study the Bible and pray together. It all sounded terrifying and quite daunting – I didn't know the first thing about the Bible or praying out loud. But over the months to come she and I kept meeting up to discuss various passages, and to pray about what we had learnt and about things going on in our lives. It was a great chance to ask all those questions that I felt embarrassed to ask my friends, who'd all been Christians for ages, like what is 'grace' and 'mercy'. And it was wonderful to begin learning directly from God's word, what he wanted for my life and being taught to look there for answers and encouragement.

The structure of the book

The book starts with a biblical basis for one-to-one work and the reasons why this type of ministry with individuals is so crucial. It then covers a number of points to consider before getting involved in one-to-one work, such as the time and personal character required and dangers to be noted and avoided. Chapter 3 looks at the three core ingredients of one-to-one work: prayer, Bible study and friendship. Chapters 4 and 5 go on to give very practical advice on how to organise meeting regularly with someone for one-to-one; options of what to study together; how to prepare and lead a Bible study; praying together; and training.

The fact that there are two chapters focussed on the 'how to' of Bible study and proportionately less material focussing on prayer and friendship is not meant to make a statement about the relative value this book places on these three elements of one-to-one work. This book strongly advocates that one-to-one work should be more than just Bible study. Chapter 3 does argue that the Bible should be at the heart of such ministry, given that it is God's authoritative word to us, but that genuine friendship and concern, as well as deep prayerfulness and dependence on God to work, should also be non-negotiable ingredients of effective one-to-one work.

There are a number of reasons for the balance of material on Bible study in this book. The first is due to the amount of good books available on prayer and the relative dearth of good accessible material on how to prepare and lead Bible studies. The second is that there is only a certain amount to be said about the subject of friendship, as, once the principles are laid out, it is very much a matter of personality and circumstances. The third and perhaps biggest reason for this balance of material is to stress that Bible study shouldn't be an optional part of an ongoing one-to-one commitment, but remain absolutely central, and that it is worth spending time working at Scripture for oneself rather than always relying on other resources to help one understand a passage. In this way, many more church members will be better equipped to wrestle with God's word for themselves and to teach it to others.

Chapter 6 covers meeting with people on an occasional or more informal basis than the regular one-to-one commitment outlined in the previous chapters. This chapter aims to encourage conversations which point each other back to the Lord Jesus and talk naturally about the joys and challenges of following him, so we can help one another live for God and for eternity.

Chapter 7 covers the potentially tricky subjects of accountability, confidentiality, pastoral issues and moving on from a commitment to meet regularly for one-to-one to a less structured friendship.

Chapter 8 aims to provide helpful resources for one-to-one work in the form of sample study material or references to other study material and books to read and recommend. It also includes the contact details of a number of counselling organizations, if such help is needed.

Final note

One last thing to say before you read this book: one-to-one work is not an exact science! It is not simply a matter of meeting the requirements, getting the right person, plugging in the right combination of prayer, Bible study and friendship, and waiting for a perfectly matured Christian to emerge, ready to repeat the process with others! It is the same with evangelism – telling someone the good news of Jesus as clearly as is possible will not mean they automatically repent and believe. There is the mystery of God's sovereignty and human choice at work determining the outcome. As one questionnaire respondent worried, 'We need to be careful that we don't slide down into a conveyor belt mentality, whereby a young Christian comes into my one-to-one circle, I pull all the right levers and do my standard "one-to-one thing" and out pops a pristine discipled Christian! We're not in the business of producing clones.'

1

What is One-to-One Work?

1. Definitions

'One-to-one' work is a catchall name for a great variety of Christian ministry with individuals. It can refer to regular Bible study going on for a couple of years or the occasional chat after a Sunday service or talking while doing the washing-up with kids hanging off you! It can apply to meeting up with a non-Christian, a new Christian, a struggling Christian, a potential Christian leader, or someone who has been going strong in their faith for years. It might involve looking at a psalm together, doing an in-depth study of a passage from 2 Timothy, reading a Christian book, talking about the sermon or sharing what God has been teaching you through a recent trial. The common factor in one-to-one work is the idea of pointing someone to Jesus, to encourage them to trust and obey the gospel of Christ.

For the purposes of this book, we have defined one-to-one work as *one Christian taking the initiative with another individual to help them know Christ better and obey Him more fully, through studying Scriptures, prayer (for and with them) and sharing one's life with them – and leaving the results to God.*

Ideally, one-to-one ministry should be of mutual encouragement to both individuals as they learn from God together. The norm in this type of friendship, however, is for one person to have more knowledge and experience as a Christian from which the other person can learn. Meeting with a more mature Christian one-to-one can help speed up and deepen the growth process of a younger Christian. Such specific individual help and encouragement can be especially helpful for those who come to Jesus after adolescence, when they have grown up into an entirely worldly set of values that have to be 'unlearned' as a new Christian. In such instances, one-to-one Bible teaching, encouragement and prayer can greatly accelerate the laying down of biblical foundations for a lifetime of discipleship.

Other terms for one-to-one ministry

Reading with someone

Have you ever heard the phrase 'are you reading with anyone at the moment'? What does it mean? Studying Shakespeare with a group of friends? Teaching someone how to read? In certain Christian circles, it simply refers to studying the Bible with a younger Christian and helping them to grow in their faith. It's just what we are talking about when we mention 'meeting regularly for one-to-one' in this book.

'Discipling' (or making disciples)

David Watson, an evangelist from the second half of the last century commented on the idea of making disciples:

> A disciple is a follower of Jesus. He has committed himself to Christ, to walking in Christ's way, to living Christ's life and to sharing Christ's love and truth with others. The verb *to disciple* describes the process by which we encourage another person to be such a follower of Jesus; it means the methods we use to help that person to become mature in Christ and so be in a position where he or she can now disciple someone else.[2]

Mentoring or coaching

These terms come mainly from the States and are generally focused on men. The aim of mentoring can be quite broad, where the mentor helps their 'protege' to realise their life's goals and grow socially, emotionally and spiritually.

'It's in this context [of mentoring] that men can share personal struggles, seek guidance, find spiritual direction and hammer out nitty-gritty issues of life.' Also, 'Mentoring is a ministry of multiplication. Every time you build into the life of another man, you launch a process that ideally will never end.'[3]

Personal work

This phrase generally refers to a less structured, more informal ministry of being concerned for the spiritual welfare of an individual and is often used in children's camp/summer venture settings or in the encouragement of Bible study group members.

2. Biblical basis

The 'one another' commands

In the New Testament we find many instructions and commands on how we are to help each other as Christians. They are sometimes called the 'one another commands' as they call us to act towards one another in a certain way. Here are some of them.

- Love one another (Jn. 13:34).
- Instruct one another (Rom. 15:14).
- Have concern for one another (1 Cor. 12:25).

- Speak the truth in love to one another (Eph. 4:15).
- Build one another up by what you say (Eph. 4:29).
- Teach and admonish one another with the word of Christ (Col. 3:16).
- Encourage one another and build one another up (1 Thess. 5:1).
- Encourage one another daily so that you are not hardened by sin's deceitfulness (Heb. 3:13).
- Spur one another on to love and good deeds (Heb. 10:24).
- Confess your sins to each other (Jas. 5:16).
- Pray for one another (Jas. 5:16; also Eph. 6:18).
- Use your gifts to serve one another (1 Pet. 3:7–10).

As we look at all these commands together, we get a strong picture of the Christian life as something essentially corporate – God's plan is that we live and grow as Christians *together*. But this only happens as we each focus on other individuals, seeking to help, encourage, teach and so on. Sadly, we are often rather poor at this.

Our relationships with other Christians so easily end up focusing on sport, home improvements, or the latest disaster with our children, rather than on Christ. The one-to-one work described in this book is designed to help us change this state of affairs and lead us to put into practice these 'one another' commands. One-to-one work can help us do that simply because we act intentionally and proactively to arrange to meet with someone to study the Bible and talk about being Christians. There is nothing strictly biblical about some of the specifics we will suggest, e.g. meeting once a week for an hour or so. And indeed, the people involved best decide those specifics. However, the overall thrust of one-to-one work will lead us to be more thoroughly biblical in our relationships as we teach and care for 'one another'.

Biblical examples to follow

In addition to one-to-one work being a good way of practising various commands in the Bible, we also see it modelled in the Bible and given as an example to follow.

When we look at how Jesus spent his three years of ministry we discover an unusual strategy. While God's intention is clearly to reach the world with the gospel, Jesus deliberately focuses on a group of only twelve, e.g. Mark 3:13–19. True, he often preached to large crowds, but he often took steps to try and avoid them too, e.g. Mark 1:43–45. What Jesus really concentrated on was teaching the twelve – and often only three of them, Peter, John and James – giving them the detailed explanation that the crowd didn't hear, e.g. Mark 4:10–34. He focused on their individual tuition and personal learning, rather than affecting a bigger group of people at a shal-lower level. Jesus' strategy for reaching the world was to first reach a small group in a thorough way – so that in time through them he would then reach the world.

We see a similar strategy when we look at Paul's ministry. Paul carried on his work of teaching and evangelism with various companions helping him. It is noticeable that those companions aren't there simply to help with the workload or carry Paul's bags, but that Paul is training them to do ministry themselves. We see this in Paul's friendship with Timothy. Having met Timothy he encourages him to accompany him (Acts 16:1–3). Timothy then travels with Paul, joining in the work. We see a similar situation with Titus (2 Cor. 2:13; 7:6ff).

Some years later Paul leaves Timothy in Ephesus (1 Tim. 1:3), and Titus in Crete (Tit. 1:5). They have become mature enough as Christians and leaders under Paul's tuition for them to work on their own now. However, Paul doesn't abandon them. As we read Paul's letters to them (1 and 2 Timothy; Titus) we see him continuing to focus on these individuals: teaching, training and encouraging them. But of course he does so for the good of the whole church. The point of the strategy he follows is that focusing on a few individuals is the best way to reach the many.

In fact Paul even commands Timothy to follow this example: 'And the things you have heard from me say in the presence of many witnesses entrust to reliable men who will also be qualified to teach others' (2 Tim. 2:2). Paul thinks Timothy should best spend his time focusing on individuals too – who in turn will teach others.

This is God's economy – to reach the many by working through the few. Or as we said at the start, the kingdom of God grows an individual at a time. It's important to be clear about this strategy as it would be easy to think that one-to-one work is a form of favouritism, picking on certain individuals at the expense of others. But that isn't the idea at all. The strategy is that by concentrating on an individual, they are helped to grow, and in turn they are able to help others. Focusing on individuals in the short term helps the greatest number of people in the long term.

3. Aims

It will help us to think biblically about one-to-one work if we begin by setting it in the context of God's plan for the universe. We will then look at some short to medium term goals that work towards this ultimate purpose.

Overall aim

Ephesians 1 reminds us that God's grand plan for the universe is to bring all things under Christ's Lordship, for the praise of his glorious name.

> *Praise be* to the God and Father of our Lord Jesus Christ, who has blessed us in the heavenly realms with every spiritual blessing in Christ. For he chose us in him before the creation of the world to be holy and blameless in his sight. In love he predestined us to be adopted as his sons through Jesus Christ, in accordance with his pleasure and will – *to the praise of his glorious grace,* which he has freely given us in the One he loves. In him we have redemption through his blood, the forgiveness of sins, in accordance with the riches of God's grace that he lavished on us with all wisdom and understanding. And he made known to us the mystery of his will according to his good pleasure, which he purposed in Christ, to be put into effect when the times will have reached their fulfilment – *to bring all things in heaven and on earth together under one head, even Christ.*
>
> In him we were also chosen, having been predestined according to the plan of him who works out

> everything in conformity with the purpose of his will, in order that we, who were the first to hope in Christ, might be *for the praise of his glory*. And you also were included in Christ when you heard the word of truth, the gospel of your salvation. Having believed, you were marked in him with a seal, the promised Holy Spirit, who is a deposit guaranteeing our inheritance until the redemption of those who are God's possession – *to the praise of his glory*.
>
> Eph. 1:3–14, my emphasis

If we look at the flow of this passage we can see that Paul starts with individuals receiving the many blessings of being saved. But this is part of the bigger aim of bringing everything under Christ. This in turn has a further aim of God being glorified. All this will reach its fulfilment when Jesus comes again, but God is working now to bring individuals to submit to Christ's rule before he comes in judgement when unrepentant sinners will be forced to acknowledge his Lordship. If this is what God is doing in the world, then obviously any involvement God allows us in his amazing plans and purposes should be done with this same aim. The ultimate goal of all Christian ministry should be the *extension of God's kingdom to the ends of the earth* (all things brought under Christ's rule) *so that God might be glorified*.

Getting there – short to medium term aims

Individuals

The first step towards this goal is for sinners to repent and bow the knee to Christ – that is, to become Christians. We need to be sharing the good news of forgiveness through Christ with those who do not acknowledge God's rule in their lives. This work of *witnessing to non-Christians* involves teaching and modelling the gospel to them, and praying for them.

The second step in bringing all things under Christ's rule is to *grow Christians in their faith* – helping them to stand firm in Jesus and mature to be more like him. We will want them to have a growing and lasting faith so that they are standing in Christ on the last day and have helped others to do so as well.

This is what Paul wanted for Christians: 'So then, just as you received Christ Jesus as Lord, continue to live in him, rooted and built up in him, strengthened in the faith, as you were taught, and overflowing with thankfulness' (Col. 2:6–7). This idea of being rooted and built up in Christ may sound simple but has enormous implications. The person who has such a growing and lasting faith has their sense of security and identity increasingly founded in Christ and nowhere else (e.g. religious works or experience, wealth, image, success, career, morality, happiness, etc.) and will be marked by a thankfulness for all that the Lord Jesus has done for them. They will also have a deepening love for God, for his word, for other Christians and for the perishing world. Such love will work itself out in self-sacrificial service of others. The person rooted in Christ will also have a confident and eager hope in the future inheritance won for them in Christ. They will wait patiently for this inheritance and not put their hope in the things of this life or in themselves (Col. 1:11–12,23).

What all this means in practice for us is that we should desire to help the individuals grow in their personal relationship with the Lord Jesus, as they get to know him better through his word and as they learn to pray. We should long for them to grow in their love for the Scriptures and in their Bible-handling skills so that they are motivated and enabled to do daily personal study and hear from God for themselves. As part of helping growth in these areas we will also be looking to address areas of confusion, certain lifestyle issues, or wrong expectations of the Christian life in a context of trust and friendship.

The church

God's purpose isn't just to save individuals, however. In Ephesians, Paul describes believers as the 'body of Christ' – as we become

Christians we join the body, God's eternal church. And God's aim is for the body to grow, to be built up ('attaining to the whole measure of the fulness of Christ', Eph. 4:13). This growth is both quantative (numbers) and qualitative (maturity and Christ-likeness). The body of Christ will grow in numbers as others are drawn to the Lord Jesus through the witness of the church in her unity and love and her teaching of the good news. The church grows in her witness as she grows in maturity as individuals are rooted and established in Christ and are motivated and equipped to serve others using their gifts.

So our work with individuals shouldn't focus only on their growth, but also on equipping them to serve others to help those people in turn to grow. We will want to help individuals to grasp the importance of being part of the body of Christ. That is, we are all given gifts with which to serve others and build them up in Christ. We will want to help our one-to-one partner to grow in their Bible-handling ability in order that they may encourage and teach others from the Scriptures. This teaching of others will normally be in informal ways ('speaking the truth in love', Eph. 4:15), such as at the end of a Sunday service or Christian Union meeting, or over a meal or coffee. However, some individuals may go on to be involved in one-to-one ministry themselves, or be involved in teaching

God's people in a more formal way. We will also want to see individuals better equipped and motivated for witnessing to non-believers – to tell others the good news that Jesus is Lord.

What's your aim?

There are many goals for one-to-one ministry that fall short of the overall aim of bringing glory to God through all things being brought under the rule of Christ. For example, maybe your ultimate aim is to:

- get someone to profess faith or get them to church/camp/Christian Union/the office prayer meeting;
- get them to know and/or be able to teach the Bible;
- encourage them to be a 'rounder'/happier/less lonely/more fulfilled person.

These may be good aims, but if we do not move beyond any of these, we are not really working for God's glory but for our agenda and temporary goals. We want people to be rooted and established in Christ, confident in their faith and growing in love and godliness as they know God better, so that the body of Christ is built up and matured as members serve one another, *so that* God, being seen and worshipped for who he really is, is glorified. Having such a high aim will mean that we are very ambitious for our one-to-one partner. We need to have eternity as our perspective and be prayerfully working their – and our – utmost for God.

These different aims can be summarized in the following diagram:

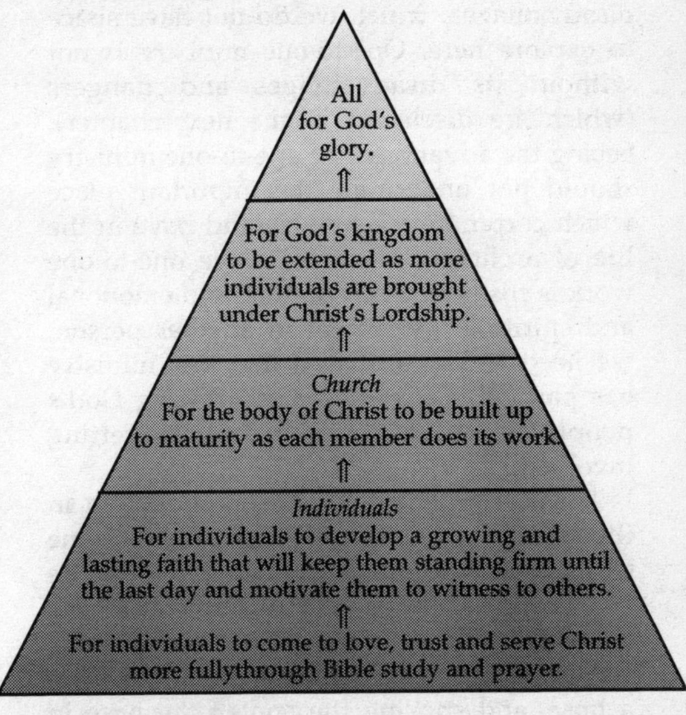

4. Advantages

In the Bible we see that God's word is to be taught to his people in many different ways:

preaching to large crowds (e.g. Acts 2:14–36); small group teaching (e.g. Acts 16:40); two-to-one teaching (e.g. Acts 18:24–26); one-to-one teaching (e.g. 1 Thess. 1:11–12); all Christians teaching one another (e.g. Col. 3:16). Each of these teaching contexts has advantages and disadvantages, which we do not have space to explore here. One-to-one ministry is not without its disadvantages and dangers (which are discussed in the next chapter). Seeing the advantages of one-to-one ministry should not undermine the important place which corporate teaching should have in the life of a church. However, since one-to-one work is costly in terms of time, and emotional and spiritual investment in another person, we need to be convinced that this ministry has particular advantages in growing God's people if we are ever to bother getting involved.

The evangelist David Watson once gave an illustration of the effectiveness of one-to-one Christian discipleship compared with more corporate teaching and discipleship. He likened it to the difference between filling a tray of bottles by spraying water at them from a hose, and sticking the end of the hose in each bottle, one at a time. Another similar illustration is that preaching is like flicking water out of a jug at a crowd; teaching in small groups is like emptying the jug into half a dozen cups; and one-to-one is like emptying the whole jug into another one.

Here are the main advantages of one-to-one work.

- *Understanding*: Studying the Bible one on one allows more time and opportunity to clarify understanding and explore doctrinal issues that a particular passage raises.
- *Application*: It can also lead to far deeper and more personal application of God's truth than can group studies or sermons.
- *Example*: It can offer a valuable opportunity for someone to see 'behind the scenes' of an older Christian's life and learn not just from their 'victories' but also failures and struggles, and to learn how to pray.
- *Accountability*: Such a friendship can offer a safe environment in which to share struggles and failures with one another.
- *Training*: This sort of relationships offers an excellent environment for ministry training.

Understanding

When you meet to study the Bible in a group setting there is limited time to tackle each person's questions or issues from the passage. The study needs to move on so that you reach the main point of the passage and have time to apply that.

A common problem in group studies is spending too much time on smaller questions raised from the text and not enough time wrestling through the big points and their implications. Over time this pattern will mean that the group aren't actually going away with what God is wanting to tell them through those passages of Scripture, but with lots of new unconnected pieces of information. This may provide lots of helpful verses for us in times of need, but it won't give us a structured, biblical worldview. It is only by reaching the theological 'punch line', the big point of the passage, that we will begin to build a right understanding of what God is saying (see also chapter 3, section 2 on the Bible).

One-to-one studies provide an excellent opportunity to spend more time addressing the individual's particular questions from the passage and really help them in their understanding of how to handle God's word correctly, without having lots of other people's issues to address at the same time. Perhaps more significantly, one-to-one studies offer more time for wrestling more thoroughly with the *big point* of the passage, without many voices clouding the issue and making for a more superficial study of the text.

Application

The second major advantage of one-to-one studies is in applying God's word to our lives. In a group setting, we are far more reluctant to open up about personal struggles – this is understandable, and some caution in what we share and with whom may be a wise thing. What is more, even if all the group were happy to be really honest and personal when it comes to applying the passage, there wouldn't be enough time for everyone to have their say. But studying a passage one-on-one is an ideal opportunity for a deep and honest wrestling with the implications of that passage. Both Christians can talk about what it would mean to apply a certain truth in their specific circumstances and then discuss why it is so hard to do this in practice. This openness will make prayer for one another so much easier and more helpful.

Some of you may well have discovered the amazing joy and privilege of seeing a younger Christian grow over weeks and months in their grasp of God's word and in Christian maturity. Sometimes this growth is barely perceptible and you have to trust that God is working faithfully 'behind the scenes' as you teach his word. At other times the change can seem obvious and dramatic, but only time will tell whether it will bear lasting fruit or not. But generally speaking, by God's grace, if the person is willing to keep meeting and learning, you will see their confidence in Jesus and the gospel of grace grow stronger as they have their doubts dealt with and struggles prayed for, and that will set them up for a lifetime of persevering faith and serving others.

Example

One-to-one ministry provides a much-needed opportunity for the Christian life of a more mature believer to be modelled to a younger Christian. This is not to say by any means that the encouragement and challenge only flow in one direction in such a relationship, but the younger Christian can often be greatly helped by seeing a more experienced disciple of Christ at closer quarters. As the older Christian shares their life – their struggles, joys, decisions, worries, encouragements in their walk with God – then the less experienced Christian can learn what it means in practice to live out God's truth in different situ-ations. It can also be a relief to find out that someone else – especially a more mature Christian – also experiences the same struggles that we do in some areas, and it can be a spur to persevere in changing. This modelling of the Christian life and of Christian ministry was key to the growth and training of the twelve apostles as Jesus lived and taught among them, and also to the likes of Paul, Timothy, Titus and Apollos.

Another area where the example of a more mature Christian is important is that of prayer. When we first become a Christian, prayer can seem quite an intimidating challenge. We may know that it is simply a matter of talking to our heavenly Father, but we still wonder what and how we are to pray. And the thought of praying out loud can be terrifying. Yet, even the twelve apostles had to be taught how to pray by Jesus (Mt. 6:7–13), and the way Jesus taught them was to pray in front of them – to model it to them. So, praying simple biblical prayers at the start and end of our time together can provide a much-needed model to the new Christian (or even non-Christian) of how to speak to God and respond to his word.

Accountability

The primary person we are all accountable to is God. However, the Bible says that we often need others to help us to see our sins and take them to God to receive the forgiveness Jesus offers. Keeping others accountable is not something we tend to be very good at, usually because we dislike others questioning our motives or actions, so we are reluctant to tackle others with such questions! But it is a very important component of church life. Colossians 3:16 says we are to teach and *admonish* one another with God's word. Admonish means to advise or urge seriously, to reprove or to warn. It is the challenge to check that someone is seeking to put God's will first in their life – and the challenge to let someone else check that for us!

One-to-one ministry can provide an excellent framework for accountability between partners. Each can be open with the other about motives, decisions, behaviour and thinking, and welcome any challenge from the other to change their ways. This in turn provides a wonderful opportunity to demonstrate and affirm grace, as you help each other to confess to God, receive forgiveness and strive to change.

Welcoming accountability

Accountability seems to be one of the key aspects in growing as a Christian and one of the key aspects that is missing from many people's lives. When I came to university I was at a stage where I had seen many of my Christian friends start off so well, but then really struggle with massive lifestyle issues, most usually relationships which resulted in them not walking with God. Being discipled by an older woman in my church was a huge help in keeping me accountable in this and so many other areas. Over time the honest and open relationship that we developed meant that as issues arose I could pray through them with her. It meant that she could ask the difficult questions and I could trust her enough to give honest answers. The security of a friendship where you know that what you say will not be gossiped about was an awesome privilege, it meant that I could tell her things while knowing she wouldn't either jump to judge me or devalue me. It all sounds pretty unreal and perhaps that's because relationships like this are no longer commonplace. They do require significant investments in time and work but are such powerful testimonies to the gospel.

Training

In many cases, the older Christian can, over time, equip their one-to-one partner to lead bible studies, give their testimony, answer difficult questions from non-believers, maybe even give a talk. In this way, we can multiply disciple-making ministry throughout the church as we train others (mainly through modelling it) to handle the Bible correctly and teach it to others. The older Christian can also encourage the new Christian to get involved in serving the church in any number of practical ways very early on.

Having laid out all these advantages of one-to-one work, they are only to be enjoyed by God's grace blessing our efforts. The testimony in the box below reminds us of the heartache of Christian ministry, when people have hard hearts which refuse to submit to Christ and his teaching.

Disappointment

Studying the Bible with others has been a great joy for me, the appointment in my week that I have most looked forward to, and that has often left me rejoicing and praising God. But it hasn't been without struggles and sadness. A few years ago I discovered that a young Christian whom I'd met with for about six months was no longer going to church; it turned out that he'd starting going out with a non-Christian, and was now sleeping with her. So I prayed, and I wrote to him. It was one of the hardest letters I've ever written, but harder still was the phone call I received a couple of days later – I still remember shaking as I held the receiver. 'Andrew, I got your letter. I don't want you ever to contact me again.' And I knew I just had to respect his choice and let him go.

Study guide

- Who were the key people who influenced you in your Christian walk? What made them so effective?
- In a sentence – or two – how you would summarize the benefits of meeting one-to-one?
- Have a read through the aims of one-to-one work given in this chapter. How might we

evaluate our meeting times in the light of these?

- Think through how one-to-one ministry can be promoted and encouraged in your church, Christian Union or work fellowship? What steps could *you* take to put it on the agenda and encourage it?

Something to do: Fix up a time to meet with your church or fellowship leader, to talk through how meeting one-to-one can be introduced or encouraged in your church, Christian Union or work fellowship. If people are already meeting me one-to-one, how could you be involved?

2

Getting Involved

1. Who me?

'But I couldn't do that, I'm not qualified in any way, I have no training or experience!' I'm sure this is how most of us feel at the thought of taking the initiative to read the Bible with a younger Christian.

Can you identify with any of the following reasons that people give for not taking the initiative with this sort of ministry?

a) It's a mystery.
No one sees it. One-to-one work is invisible to the rest of the church. We often don't know what is involved – what it looks like. And generally, no one will ask if we're doing it so it's very easy for it not to get done.

b) It feels unnatural.
It can feel very unnatural to ask someone if they'd like to meet up and study the Bible

together. The suggestion of meeting up can seem totally inappropriate because we live in a culture where such a relationship would be thought only appropriate in the context of counselling and therapy. And since it's invisible when it does happen, so that people generally don't know what it entails, the suggestion to meet up one-to-one to look at the Bible together can seem profoundly odd or suspect!

c) I feel inferior/incompetent.
Perhaps most commonly, we may feel too shy to initiate such a relationship. We may feel we can't relate to someone else's situation, perhaps because they're engaged, or in a high-powered job, and we are not, so we assume that it will be impossibly difficult to identify with them. There is the great fear of feeling out of our depth as we try and teach others. It's much easier just to say 'that's not really for me'.

Feeling inadequate for the task

Do a one-to-one with someone? I really wasn't sure that I could. Why did I lack confidence? After all, I had received good training in understanding the Bible and leading Bible studies. I had several years' experience of teaching the Bible in a group setting. But I had no personal experience of meeting up with anyone to study the Bible on a one-to-one basis. I just wasn't sure what it looked like. But then I had an opportunity I couldn't refuse.

I had got to know a girl at our church. Although she had been a Christian for some years, she really wanted to be able to understand the Bible better. 'Please will you teach me?' she said. So we arranged to meet up once a fortnight and study 1 Peter (a book I was reasonably familiar with). We both looked at the passage beforehand and I would ask questions I'd prepared. As what we were studying challenged us, we talked these things through and prayed about them. As issues in our lives came up, we talked them through and prayed about them. She was honest and open which helped me to be honest with her. This really helped us to be real with one another. I wasn't perfect – I made mistakes. We probably spent too much time chatting before getting down to our Bible study. It was hard work at times. But there's nothing like doing something to learn how to do it. I'm so glad I did. Meeting up with her was one of the most encouraging and rewarding things I did over those two years. Now my friend is herself reading the Bible with a young Christian. We still get together once a month or so to catch up and pray and encourage each other. It's been great.

d) It wouldn't be practical.
Maybe you feel you simply don't have the time or that it would be impractical due to circumstances. It might be that it is genuinely impossible to give the necessary commitment for a number of very good reasons.

The qualifications

To do one-to-one ministry there are a few requirements. Essentially you simply need to be a Christian who is holding firm to the gospel of Christ and seeking to live for God's glory. You will note that all the characteristics mentioned below are ones we can grow in. The requirements for one-to-one work do not include personality traits. We are all different – we have different natures, different tendencies, different personalities. It can be very easy to assume that we have to be 'a certain type of person' to do this work, especially if we have had it modelled to us by someone who is not like us at all. God has made us all unique and there must be complete freedom to express our uniqueness, within the bounds of the following criteria:

We must have a strong personal commitment to the Lord Jesus

Have I begun to know Jesus in the way that I want the one I'm looking after to know him? Am I making progress in my faith and growing to love him more each day? Am I a praying person? Do I seek to pray daily and in dependence in all things? We need to be living examples to those who are in our care. We don't need to be perfect or incredibly mature, by any stretch, but we need to be going in the right direction in our walk with God. This involves being honest about our failures and repenting of them, and striving to live a godly life in submission to God's word.

We will need to love

This is a requirement of all disciples of Jesus (Jn. 13:34–35). We may be nervous; we may feel ill equipped or inadequate as a Christian model, but 'love covers over a multitude of sins' (1 Pet. 4:8). Only with love will we have the right priorities for our one-to-one partner: we won't just want them to be a happy, average member of the church – we will want their highest good. Listen to Paul in Thessalonians: 'Brothers, we instructed you how to live in order to please God, as in fact you are living. Now we ask you and urge you in the Lord Jesus to do this more and more' (1 Thess. 4:1). He wants the very best for those to whom he ministers. Only with love will we serve them sacrificially to this end, will we keep praying for them, will we be patient as they forget to turn up or fail to change as hoped, will we willingly 'spend and be spent' (2 Cor. 12:15) on their behalf, giving up our time for them. We do not, of course, have this love naturally; left to ourselves, we look out for ourselves above everyone else. The only way to put someone else's good before our own is to go back to the cross and ask God to fill us with Jesus' love ('We love because he first loved us', 1 Jn. 4:19).

We will need to have a working knowledge of the Bible

The Bible is our most important tool (2 Tim. 2:15; 3:16). We will need to be convinced that God works powerfully through his word, by his Spirit, and to accept the Bible's authority on all matters on which it speaks. We will consider these ideas more in the following chapter, but suffice it to say here that we will need to have a love and respect for the Bible if we are to be involved in discipling others one-to-one. Although it would be helpful to be confident with the main doctrines of the Bible, to know the *broad outline* of God's plan of salvation in history (not all the dates and details!), and to know about the different types of literature in the Bible and how to approach them, this is not essential before you start doing one-to-one work. We don't need to be experts or have memorized hundreds of verses. There are several books that can help you prepare in this way, e.g. John Stott's *Understanding the Bible* (London: Union Scripture, 1972), David

Jackman's *I Believe in the Bible* (London: Hodder and Stoughton, 2000) or Stephen Motyer's *Opening the Bible with Pleasure* (Cambridge: Crossway Books, 1997). Chapter 5 of this book should also help with how to understand Scripture better.

We will need to be honest and simple

We love it when someone regards us as a bit of a 'guru', but this is not Christian leadership. We are trying to point others to Christ, not ourselves; we want them to see *his* glory. Therefore we will want to be honest and not put on an act. When we are struggling with something or confused by something, we will need to say so. That is not to say that we are to offload all our spiritual hang-ups and failures on them – that wouldn't be appropriate or kind to a young Christian. But neither are we to act as though we are super-spiritual, a textbook Christian. It is in our weakness that Christ is revealed more fully in us.

Related to this is the need to be simple. A young Christian does not need to hear our latest theological ideas. He or she needs the basic teachings about Christ explained in a clear way with the example of our lives to back it up. So we will need to be able to explain in normal language our favourite terms like justification, redemption, grace, even sin, and be able to pray simple, heartfelt prayers with them.

We will need to be prepared to count the cost

Any Christian ministry is costly. Rewarding, but costly. It is primarily costly in terms of our time and emotional energy, as mentioned in the above point about love. We must not go into one-to-one ministry if we are not prepared to make sacrifices in our lives in order to serve the other person as we should. Paul warns Timothy that passing on the gospel to others, who in turn can pass it on to others, will involve hardship (2 Tim. 2:1–3). Notice also what Paul says about his ministry of presenting people 'mature' in Christ: 'To this end I labour, struggling with all his energy, which works so powerfully in me' (Col. 1:29).

We should give proper consideration to being involved in this work, even if we can't do it under ideal conditions, because it can be such a wonderful mutual encouragement to both one-to-one partners. The box below describes how one mother has found it possible to meet up with another woman (without children) and has been blessed by their times together.

Even mums can do it!

In many ways I hesitate before putting anything down on paper about meeting with people one-to-one as a mother because everyone's daily routine varies so much and changes with the age and number of children. However I found that while having only one child I was able to meet up with people to read the Bible and pray, and loved being able to do so. We would arrange to meet at my house when my daughter was meant to be sleeping (although she did join us sometimes and made noisy contributions). This did mean I was unable to use that time for getting other jobs done or a quick snooze, but it helped me enormously to keep God's perspective on life during what was a wonderful, scary and stressful year, as well as being a lovely, grown-up, no nappy time!

If meeting up regularly to do one-to-one work would be completely impractical for us for some reason, then are we able to facilitate another person being involved in this work? If we know someone who has children but would like to be involved in one-to-one work, can we find childcare for them from another church member, or babysit for them ourselves? If we have the contact with someone who would like to study the Bible one-to-one, whether a Christian or an interested non-Christian, could we arrange for someone else at church to meet up with them? We can remain in touch with them and ask about their one-to-one, but without needing to make the regular commitment to meeting up.

If we commit to getting involved in one-to-one ministry, we will need to have a strong grasp of the overall aim of Christian ministry – the extension of God's kingdom for God's glory (see page 5) – to motivate us to keep serving. We also need to trust, however, that it is God's power that will enable us to keep going; Paul laboured and struggled and endured hardship with God's energy and grace. This sort of ministry with individuals is worth the cost. This is what Paul says about the Thessalonian Christians with whom he worked one-to-one while he was with them (for more see page 14): 'For now we really live, since you are standing firm in the Lord. How can we thank God enough for you in return for all the joy we have in the presence of our God because of you?' (1 Thess. 3:8–9).

2. Who with?

Perhaps the most important criterion for whom to meet with is *spiritual hunger*. If there is no hunger to hear from God and put his teaching into practice then the motivation to meet up will be one-sided and it will go nowhere. Whether the person is not yet a Christian, is a new Christian, struggling in their faith, or really going for it, you can only have a ministry with them if they are *willing* to actually meet up with you. It doesn't mean that they always have to be glowing with excitement at the prospect of the meeting and never cancel on you, but there needs to be enough interest and desire to learn and grow that you don't have to coerce them into meeting up.

Choosing someone to meet with

So often it is actually quite obvious who would be a good person to meet up with. I had been leading a Christianity Explored group and one of the girls in the group professed faith and started to get going as a Christian. When the course finished, she still had so many questions, so I invited her for lunch one day and asked if she would like to meet regularly for some Bible study and prayer. She leapt at the chance.

I think that if we are willing to do this type of ministry, then God will give us someone to meet up with, because it is such a key work. So if there isn't anyone immediately obvious then I guess you can ask one of the church leaders if they know of anyone who would value meeting up in this way. I always pray for God to give me eyes to see opportunities for someone to meet up with and encourage.

So, is there someone in your church – in your youth group, Christianity Explored or Alpha group, home group, mums and toddlers group, on the flower or coffee rota – or at the work place, in your dormitory from camp or in your college Christian Union, who would be willing to study the Bible with you? (How do you know? You ask them – and we'll think about that more in the next chapter.)

There are some key people to consider for a period of one-to-one discipleship, however:

- Interested inquirers into Christianity – those who are keen to find out more about Jesus.
- New Christians – those who have recently come to faith in the Lord Jesus.
- Those who will be able to teach others (whether as a Bible study leader in a voluntary, part-time capacity, or as a full-time, paid ministry position), who need training and equipping.

Before you approach someone about meeting one-to-one, it is best if you go and speak to the leader of your church, small group, summer camp or Christian Union, or those with a responsibility for youth or student work, about your intentions. They may be able to offer you further training, helpful advice or want to check that it is appropriate for you to be embarking on this ministry. They might also be the best people to advise you on who would benefit from meeting up with a more mature Christian and be able to make the introduction.

Appearances can be deceptive

I was fortunate to know two guys with whom I thought it would be good to read one to one, and to have the time available to do it. One seemed harder work – he had lots of doctrinal issues and was a less mature Christian; the other guy appeared keen, interested and an ideal candidate.

Looking back, appearances were deceptive. The less mature guy turned up fortnightly to study Colossians having done prep on the relevant passage beforehand. He demonstrated a desire to learn from God and to apply what he was learning to his life.

The other guy, despite his enthusiasm to meet up, rarely, if ever, did any prep and was happy just to socialize. Needless to say, with the first guy we had a mutually fruitful time listening to God speak to us in Colossians, while the sessions with the other guy petered out in the end.

Meeting with teenagers

Many of the ideas and principles expressed in this book about meeting one-to-one with adults are also applicable and appropriate to meeting one-to-one with young people. Children and young people benefit enormously from decent relationships with adults and often look beyond the home or school environment to find these relationships.

Because of the Children's Act (1989) and a number of high profile cases, there is a general suspicion about adults relating to young people. This means that we have to be wise, sensible, beyond reproach and, of course, legal in our contact with young people. Both the Church Pastoral Aid Society and The Churches' Child Protection Advisory Service have produced helpful guidelines on working with young people. Both organizations endorse the benefits of adults building relationships with young people while at the same time urging people to be sensible (see resources section).

The general principles are:

- Avoid situations where you are completely alone or unsupervised with a young person. Make sure that there are other adults around; leave doors open; let others know what you are doing.
- Make every effort to ensure that nothing that you do or say can be misread or taken the wrong way.
- Where possible avoid physical contact.

According to the Children's Act, 'appropriate' physical contact might include restraining a young person from endangering themselves or others.
- Never promise confidentiality – there are occasions where you have a legal responsibility to pass on information that you have received from a young person.

How many to meet with?

If we are so convinced that one-to-one is a vital ministry to be involved in, shouldn't we try to meet with as many people as we can squeeze into our diaries? The simple answer is no! In the next chapter we will cover what is involved in one-to-one work and we will see that it can be quite demanding of our time and emotional energy. Involvement in this sort of work is a real privilege and can be very rewarding. However, it can also be very challenging and even draining. This is, to a certain extent, part of the inevitable cost of being involved in Christian ministry, but there is a point at which it is wise to say 'no' to opportunities for the sake of the long-term sustainability of one's ministry. Women most commonly report feeling over-burdened emotionally (which can lead to physical exhaustion) through trying to commit to too many friendships. We should not over-commit but take on one person initially and see how that works out. We should be careful to maintain other close friendships for accountability and encouragement (see chapter 7) since one-to-one arrangements can be short-term and don't nec-essarily result in a life-long, close friendship.

If you are in a position where you have quite a bit of spare time to give to gospel work, then it might be a great use of that time to meet one-to-one with more individuals. If you are working or a busy student or mother, then committing to meet up with one individual over the space of a few months or even a year or two is a wonderful thing and is a great investment for the whole church.

Women often need more time

When I worked for a church as a lay assistant, I became aware that, while I could easily see a guy, catch up, read the Bible and pray with him in forty minutes, the female lay assistant often needed much longer when she met with the women, and if she only gave someone forty minutes they sometimes felt resentment.

3. Potential dangers

We saw in the last chapter how many advantages one-to-one ministry can have in helping people to grow in their trust in and obedience to the gospel, leading to the whole church being built up in maturity and God being glorified. One-to-one discipleship does, however, pose a number of potential dangers, which may be one of the reasons why so little of this ministry happens. Behind most of these dangers is the fear of cult-like 'heavy shepherding' or manipulation. These dangers of one-to-one work, while not inevitable, are very important to be aware of, and to watch out for.

Intensity

When two people meet together regularly and share their deepest spiritual and possibly emotional struggles and fears as they study God's word and pray together, there is always the danger of an unhealthy intensity developing in the relationship. At the most obvious level this means that one-to-one ministry should always be between two people of the same sex, especially where one (or both) is married (to someone else) and/or one is not a Christian. Although it wouldn't necessarily be wrong for a romantic relationship to develop as a result of two single Christians of the opposite sex meeting together like this, it might be quite a distraction – minds might not always be focused on a growing relationship with God!

In addition, however, we must not be naïve about the dangers of homosexual temptation that might develop in a same-sex discipleship relationship. If that is a struggle for you, you must make sure that a church leader knows about it and is happy to look out for you before you embark on one-to-one ministry. You should also take care not to meet with someone who you know shares the same struggles lest you put yourself in a vulnerable situation. With those safeguards, you are not necessarily excluded from this kind of ministry.

The conclusion is that, although meeting regularly to study and apply the Bible and pray together is highly personal, it is wise to be cautious about the level of intensity that develops in and outside those meetings. All of the following points are linked to this point.

Control

This is where one person, usually the initiator, tries to manipulate and control the other for a number of possible reasons. Steve Wookey, in his book *When a church becomes a cult*, quotes Jerry Jones from his research of the Boston Church of Christ. This is what he says on their practice of discipling:

> A disciple is one who obeys his discipler even if he doesn't comprehend what he's told. Because he wants to have a teachable heart, he will fully obey and be totally obedient even if what he's asked to do is contrary to what he would

> normally do or think. To distrust the person God had put in his life is equal to distrusting God and his faith in God is shown by his faith in his discipler.[4]

One of the marks of cults is that the 'discipler' in the one-to-one relationship holds a position of great authority over the 'disciple'. The younger convert is encouraged to submit to their discipler in all matters, for their own good. It is impossible, however, to give the impression that I am important and that Christ is important at the same time. If he is to become greater, then 'I must become less'. Yet one-to-ones can provide a great opportunity for me to look important. The position of spiritual guru appeals to our pride. Unless we watch ourselves, a relationship in which we are supposed to serve a younger Christian can all too easily become one where we lord it over them, or even manipulate and control them, for the sake of our own ego. Richard Bewes Rector of All Souls, Langham Place, comments on this issue in the box below.

Disciples of but one man

Any aspect of control is a dangerous root to watch out for in any one-to-one ministry. I remember once sensing it very early on in someone 'targeting' me for personal work and it was utterly off-putting and resulted in me avoiding him at all costs because I didn't want to feel forced into meeting up with him. I felt he didn't really care about who I was or where I was at but that he had an agenda that I just wasn't ready for. He launched straight in there with where I was going wrong and what I needed to learn and I felt the Bible was being forced on me.

Control and a misplaced sense of authority can be a very dangerous thing. I have learnt over the years that the most important thing in personal work is to get people to be disciples of *but one man* – and that is Christ not me! This means it is a ministry of coming alongside people, not over them, and both growing in our walk with the Lord side by side.

Legalism

This is probably the most common and insidious danger of one-to-one ministry. Concern for personal godliness can easily spill over into rules and regulations being imposed on the younger Christian, usually unintentionally. David Watson comments, 'The pressures may not be structural but emotional. Through the genuine and detailed care of mature Christians, those under their pastoral care ... can feel strong emotional ties that are not easy to break

... Strong loyalties are established, so that any deviation can seem like rebellion.' The one being 'discipled' can feel immense internal or external pressure to please their 'discipler' and not disappoint them. Good works become linked to people-pleasing and are no longer solely about a grateful response to God for all he has done for us. The older Christian must be very aware of this danger and keep pointing to Jesus in all things, being open about the failures in their own life and their thankfulness for forgiveness.

Avoiding guru status!

I had been meeting with a girl for a year when it became apparent that she was looking to me as the expert question answerer! If a friend asked her a question she wouldn't answer but would wait until I was available to come and speak to the friend myself. I realized that we needed to work on looking to the Bible for the answers and on trusting God that she could be used by him with her friends and she didn't need an 'expert' by her side.

Over-dependence

This can happen where one person is less mature or secure either spiritually or emotionally or on both fronts, and looks to the stronger one for direction, strength and confidence where they should be looking to God for all these things. Commonly the younger Christian can end up depending on the older one for answers to any difficult questions, for guidance on decisions and affirmation of their choices and their whole walk with God.

Pride

How easily pride slips in if we are being treated as spiritual 'gurus' and being depended on in all sorts of ways! Pride can also take hold of us when we are privileged enough to see real fruit in the other person's life and congratulate ourselves on what a great job we've done of discipling them! We must remember that it is God's work to change people (see the section on prayer, pp.17-18). Remembering this will also prevent us from becoming burdened with worry or guilt when we don't see the fruit we long for in our one-to-one partner or when they are demanding much more out of the friendship than we are able to give. Pride will mean we depend far too much on our own abilities, and not enough on God's power, in order to achieve the aims of one-to-one work.

Giving the glory to God not me

A danger I have noticed in my own one-to-one work is that of becoming proud. I would be pleased when people noticed that someone I met with was growing – which in itself isn't bad, but I realized that I was taking the credit for their growth, in my heart if not explicitly. I thought it reflected well on me that the person had been growing. This takes all the glory away from God and puts it onto me – it is an attitude that I constantly have to battle with.

Isolation

This can happen where the initiator, for whatever reason, takes the other person out of the church family so that their one-to-one meeting becomes the main focus of the other's Christian life. We need to make sure that the individual we meet up with is fully committed to and involved in serving the broader church and being encouraged by them.

There can be real dangers when individuals decide that they would rather just meet up with one or two other Christians for their prime source of teaching and Christian encouragement. God has purposed that we are to be born into and grow up in a Christian church family. He has given each of his children specific gifts with which to serve the other members of the family so that every Christian is, in fact, needed for the whole body of the believers to grow. We are interdependent on one another so there is no room for 'private' churches. All one-to-one work needs to feed individuals into the wider church family so they may be integrated into the local body of believers through serving and being served.

Avoiding these dangers

These dangers can mostly be avoided when we are aware of them and are cautious, prayerful and accountable in our ministry. Chapter 7 'Other Considerations' outlines the need for the person initiating a one-to-one relationship with another to be accountable to someone outside that friendship. However, perhaps the biggest help in avoiding these dangers in one-to-one ministry is seeing the importance of the local church.

What Rico Tice learnt

I do remember a placement in Sydney, Australia, when the evangelist I was shadowing rightly admonished me for not trusting the local church to look after the individuals I had done one-to-one with. I had been running a private church and the pressure of it was overwhelming me. I now work much harder at integrating those I read the Bible with into the local church. If I try to be the local church to individuals I'll collapse.

Study guide

- What reasons can you give for not getting involved in one-to-one? Are they insurmountable?
- With reference to 'the qualifications' listed, which areas do you think you might need to strengthen? Would your church leaders agree with you? Would those weak areas stop you getting started – or will practice make you better?
- Taking each of the 'Dangers' listed, think through how we can take steps to avoid each one.
- Richard Bewes is quoted in this chapter saying that the most important thing in personal work is for people to be 'disciples of but one man – Jesus'. How are we tempted to forget that – both consciously and unconsciously?

Something to do: Go and ask a friend or Christian leader to comment on your suit-abil-ity for reading one-to-one with someone. Ask them to state what specific areas you might need to work on, and ask them how they can help you with this.

3

What's Involved?

1. Prayer

The key to all Christian service is prayer. However good a friend we are, however faithful and thorough our studies are and however wise our advice is, we cannot produce fruit in someone's life that will last for eternity by our own efforts. It is *God's work* to bring people to new life in Christ and it is *God's work* to continue that good work until the last day (Phil. 1:6). It is the work of God's Spirit to produce his fruit in us (Gal. 5:22–23) – the character of Christ. So we need to be crying out to God to be establishing and growing his children according to his good will. We must be utterly dependent on him to work his perfect will in people's lives, rather than depending on our methods or commitment to change people in a lasting way.

It is indeed possible to change people by pressure, manipulation or even inspiration, but this change is usually temporary and not necessarily in the right direction. Such change creates dependency on someone other than the Lord Jesus Christ, and instead, as we have said before, we are to be disciples of but one man.

So what sort of things should we be praying? Well, a good place to start is to look at what Paul prays for the churches in his letters. Don Carson has written an outstanding book (*A Call to Spiritual Reformation* [Leicester: IVP, 1992]), on how we can learn from Paul's priorities in his prayers. It is an excellent book to read if you are thinking about getting involved in discipling others. Paul was very thankful to God for those he was sharing the Gospel with. However, he continued to pray for these key things for them:

- Spiritual understanding and wisdom – to better know God's *will* (his plan, the gospel) and God's *love* and our *hope* (see Eph. 1:17–19; 3:14–19; Phil. 1:9; Col. 1:9).
- Godly/righteous living (see Phil. 1:9–11; Col. 1:10; 2 Thess. 1:12).
- Power/strengthening (for understanding, godliness and endurance) (see Eph. 1:19; Col. 1:11; 2 Thess. 2:16–17).
- Thankfulness, prayerfulness and joy (see Eph. 6:18; Phil. 4:4–7; 1 Thess. 5:16–18).

- Love for one another (see 1 Thess. 3:12).
- For Christ to be glorified in us (see 2 Thess. 1:12).
- Anything else we might be anxious about (see Phil. 4:6–7).

How often should we say such prayers then? As often as we are able! Don't we all struggle with our prayer lives? This is where the world, the flesh and the devil want to hinder us most, because prayer is at the very heart of our relationship with God and has eternal significance. Paul describes Epaphras as 'always wrestling in prayer' for his fellow Colossians (Col. 4:12). It can feel like a real battle to get down to praying for others, and in fact the Bible tells us that we are engaged in a spiritual battle (Eph. 6:10–18). As Paul reaches his conclusion of how to be prepared for this battle against 'the devil's schemes', he says, 'And pray in the Spirit on all occasions with all kinds of prayers and requests. With this in mind, be alert and always keep on praying for all the saints.' It's quite a challenge, isn't it! Belief in the reality of the battle and the urgency of the need and a genuine love for others are what is needed to keep us praying. We need to keep meditating on the Scriptures (see Appendix) and asking God for help, to increase our faith and love.

Here are a few practical things that can help us in our prayer life:

- Prayer lists/diaries that allocate certain people (or countries, mission organizations, areas of ministry and so on) to each day of the week or month.
- Meditating on a thought for the day and praying that through for others (see Appendix).
- Using Paul's prayers to guide your intercessions.
- Prayer partnerships – regularly meeting up with a friend for accountability and prayer (see chapter 7).

2. Bible study

Go into any bookshop the world over, and you'll find no shortage of self-help books: *How to be Rich and Famous*, *Bringing up Teenagers*, *The Successful Marriage*. A glance through the Amazon.com 100 bestsellers shows the list to be dominated by this sort of reading. But it's not just bookshops that can offer endless advice – how about the advice so readily and freely dispensed by your colleagues in the coffee break, by fellow students in the union bar, by grannies in their armchairs, and mothers at the playgroup? What's more, much of this advice is sincerely and honestly given.

As children, didn't we all love chocolate and sweets? Given the choice most of us would have eaten them all day. Down with vegetables, up with sugar and chocolate! Our worldview was so narrow and it was all about the here and now. Our parents, however, had a bigger view of the world. They knew we'd grow, and to grow we'd need a varied diet – and teeth to eat with! Their 'bigger picture' of the world informed their view of what our diet needed to be.

As Christians we've been given the full picture of what life is about. Life is not merely about the here and now, but also, and more significantly, an eternity with Jesus. People need to know these truths and then build their lives around them. Going back to Paul's aim in his ministry in Colossians 1:28, we also see how he sets about achieving it: 'We proclaim him, *admonishing and teaching everyone with all wisdom,* so that we may present everyone perfect in Christ' (my emphasis).

That's our challenge. Our tool, according to the verse, is 'all wisdom'. Where can we find such wisdom, which ultimately will lead people to become 'perfect in Christ', able to keep going until the last day? In this section, we make the case that the only place where we can find this wisdom, with its eternal perspective, is the Bible.

'Just teach the Bible'

One of my first experiences of reading the Bible with someone was with a young man on the verge of giving up his faith. He'd returned from a gap year only to discover that his dad, his great Christian role model, had a few months ago left his family to live with another woman. My friend was devastated; it came as a massive blow to him both emotionally and spiritually. I felt totally out of my depth and at a loss as to how to help him – what did I know about depression, about counselling, about that kind of psychological turmoil? But then an older friend in the church gave me some advice: 'Just teach him the Bible, Andrew, that's your job. Teach him the Bible.' And so that's what I did, week by week. It looked pretty unspectacular at the time; there were times I doubted whether it would be enough. Yet it kept him a Christian. And it changed him, little by little. Today, he among all my friends is one who lives for Jesus. 'Teach him the Bible, Andrew.' It was good advice, that.

The Bible is God's true word

The work of putting ink on paper in the Bible was of course that of men – there are sixty-six books in it, written by forty authors, covering at least one thousand six hundred years. 2 Peter 1:20–21 tells us that this is not the whole story. Men put words on paper, but God *inspired* them to write, carrying them along through the work of the Holy Spirit. So when we read the Bible we are reading words inspired by God – his words. This point is affirmed in 2 Peter 3:15 – Paul wrote, but God gave him the wisdom. (For more on the authority of Scripture as God's revealed word, read John Stott's *Understanding the Bible* [London: Scripture Union, 1972].)

The implications of this are profound. It's a truth that makes the Bible far superior to any other source of wisdom. The words of the 'author and perfecter of our faith' are readily available to one and all. He is our creator – he knows us and loves us better than anyone. If we want to understand how to get right with God, surely this is the book to use. The words of a head of state are laced with informed wisdom, but getting daily access to a head of state is not possible. With the Bible, we can have daily access to the king of kings, the one who is the source of all wisdom.

When we have understood that it is God who has written the Bible, we can begin to appreciate some of its worth to us. Any self-help book, or advice offered in the canteen, is offered at arm's length – the people offering it have not made us, so can't fully understand us. Nor is their love for us complete and unrelenting – even the love we have for our children or spouses can have constraints.

But if we look at God, we see someone who not only knows us, but also made us. He not only made us, but also loves us so much that he sent his Son to die for us. So when he speaks, surely we will want to hear what he says? Throughout history he has shown a deep concern for me. As my maker, he knows what is best for me – and most amazingly, when I have messed up, he has offered me a way back. So if God has inspired this book, we should want to read it, and introduce others to it. The Bible is the most significant love letter of all time – so it should be read, and read by all to whom it was written, not just a limited few. Not only read, but cherished.

We can have great confidence as we read this personal letter to us from God, knowing that every word of it is true. As we mentioned before, there is a great hunger these days for self-help and 'personal development' resources. There is a plethora of training tapes, books or evening classes to choose from. It is difficult to know how useful these are until you try them, and even then it may be years before you can see whether what you have learned has had any worth. But the Bible has infinite worth, because the Bible is true.

Proverbs 30:5 tells us that 'Every word of God is flawless.'

With so many options for guidance and personal development, how reassuring it is to offer those in our care the Bible – every word in it is flawless. That can't be said of other options. That's not to say that from time to time we might come across things in the Bible that look flawed – things that might appear old – fashioned, wrong or contradictory. When that happens, the first thing to do is go back to Proverbs 30:5. If God's words are flawless, then it's us – collectively as human beings – who are getting it wrong when we think the Bible has got it wrong.

The Bible has the answers

I remember doing my first lot of prep for a one-to-one meeting, spending five minutes reading the passage and then going to a concordance to find out what it meant! I was found out! The year I spent 'reading' with an older Christian at my church was hugely helpful in opening my eyes as to how to study the Bible, how to understand the Bible for myself and how to apply the Bible. As we studied and shared, I was challenged on how much of my thinking was not necessarily of a biblical origin, and how the Bible was the authority that I needed to submit to. Additionally, and perhaps most significantly, I remember how time and time again, as issues cropped up in my own life the Bible provided the answer. As I dealt with different situations I faced, it was right to apply the Biblical principles I had been learning. Gradually, in conversations with others, it wasn't my personal opinion I was giving, and not even the opinion of the person who was discipling me, but rather God's opinion, as I discovered it through his word. What a privilege it was to have someone invest in me, and guide me in Bible study, in knowing God better and in applying what I was learning.

The Bible is God's designated tool for one-to-one work

God is in the business of bringing people into a relationship with him, and not only that, but bringing his people into maturity in that relationship. As our loving Father, joining him in that work should be our first concern. He has not left us without a tool for that job. 2 Timothy 3:15–16 tells us what that designated tool is – the Bible! Paul writes, '… from infancy you have known the holy Scriptures, which are able to make you wise for salvation through faith in Christ Jesus. All Scripture is God-breathed and is useful for teaching, rebuking, correcting and training in righteousness.'

These two verses tell us a number of things we can expect to achieve through regular dependence on the Bible in our one-to-one times. First of all, verse 15 shows us that the Scriptures are 'able to make [us] wise for salvation'. In some cases we will be meeting up with a non-believer, and our first concern will be for them to be wise for salvation, and have 'faith in Christ Jesus'. The Bible is the book to give them the wisdom to discern that faith. We should use it unashamedly and extensively to prove that Jesus is Lord and explain God's plan of salvation. Sometimes non-believers will challenge us on the authority of the book, and we may be tempted to give up on the Bible in our attempts to convince them. But if it is salvation we want for our one-to-one partners, this is the book that we must stick to, since it is 'able' to bring them to that point.

Verse 16 makes perhaps the boldest statement in the Bible about the nature and purpose of these Scriptures. It begins by asserting the divine authorship of the Bible – a point we covered above – but then goes on to explain what we can do with it. The first thing is teaching. We will have much ground to cover with our one-to-one partners as we seek to teach them doctrine about God, his plan for salvation, us and the world. As times change, ideas on all these subjects change too. The temptation might be to pick up the latest trendy book on any of these matters – and sometimes that can be a useful thing to do, especially if a particular area is of special interest or difficulty. But our final authority must remain the Bible. What we teach people, they are likely to pass on, so if our teaching is wrong, the untruths can be multiplied. This was a point Paul knew well when he stressed to Timothy the need to pass on pure doctrine (1 Tim:3–4).

Next we find that the Bible is useful for 'rebuking and correcting'. A fuller description of how we should do this very careful work of rebuking and correcting can be found in chapter 6. The key thing to stress is that we must not force our own agendas onto people and rebuke and correct them if they are not living up to those agendas. The best way to 'rebuke and correct' is to do as the verse says, and use the Bible to do the work! If we are using the Bible humbly and clearly, and adopting a widely accepted biblical interpretation, the message is much more likely to have a positive reception. Without the Bible, rebuke and correction has no authority, and can rightly be ignored.

Lastly we read that the Bible is useful for 'training in righteousness'. This means encouraging the people we meet with to take a good look at their own lives and work on cutting out sin. They should take 1 Timothy 4:16 to heart – watching both their life and doctrine closely. If our one-to-one partner has truly grasped the central doctrines of the Christian faith then godly living should flow out of that. Sometimes, however, the applications of doctrine may need to be worked through more carefully, or are perhaps not immediately apparent. Greater experience in Christian things can be invaluable to the young Christian in this respect.

Having our confidence in God's word to work in people's lives means we're not moralizing – 'you must do this, don't do that, repent and do the right thing'! Nor is it 'psychologizing', which just focuses on feelings – 'the reason you're living like this is because you lack self-esteem and therefore need to feel better about yourself'. Both of these approaches are shallow – they fail to account for sin and they don't relate to the gospel.

This is very different from much secular counselling which treats us as god – we're in charge; we need to be enabled to take control of our lives and the situation we find ourselves in. The gospel says Jesus Christ is God and he alone is in control. Jesus compares himself to a good shepherd who looks after and leads the flock – we should want people to come under his care and rule. Behavioural problems can often be symptoms of sin and not believing the gospel – whether moral issues like anger, lying, lust, or personality problems such as insecurity or arrogance. The danger is that we hive these issues off into a department called 'counselling' or 'therapy', and we disconnect the issues from the gospel and from Jesus Christ. You see the opposite in the New Testament letters, classically in Ephesians where the first part, chapters 1–3, deals with what God has done in Jesus Christ, and the second part is the practical application of that. The point is that all these lifestyle issues are ultimately dealt with theologically, by the gospel. It's only when we understand the gospel and the implications of the gospel that our lives are transformed. So our confidence should be in the Bible to change lives. Wherever and whatever situations our one-to-one partners are facing, the Scriptures will always be powerful. Even if we feel out of our depth, we can still be reminding people gently that God is good, in control and using every circumstance to make individuals more like Jesus.

In the UK, a brand of wood sealant was sold with the simple slogan that 'it does what it says on the tin'. 2 Timothy 3:17 says that the Bible, if used and taught correctly, will 'enable the man of God to be thoroughly equipped for every good work'. If we have used God's tool for one-to-one correctly, we will have the joy of seeing the Bible do exactly what it says in verse 17 – our one-to-one partners will be thoroughly equipped for every good work, and we will be able to pass them on into God's care with every confidence.

The Bible as a tennis racquet!

My theory is that using the Bible in personal work is like using a tennis racquet in tennis! It is totally necessary for starters. But also there is great freedom with how you use it in one-to-one work (within the boundaries of handling it correctly, of course!). As any tennis player – novice or professional – will pick up a racquet and use it in a unique way, with different types and combinations of shots, with varying strength and speed, different grips, different hands even, so we can pick up the Bible with another individual and use it in a unique way to fit our different gifts, personalities and circumstances. There is great freedom with that one constant – the indispensable equipment for the activity.

3. Friendship

There is a great lack of committed friendships in our culture today. It is part of the demise of long-term community relationships. Many people are crying out for friends who will 'stick closer than a brother' and instead seeking comfort and support through therapy or counselling or even Internet chat rooms. Alice Fryling, in her book *The Disciplemakers' Handbook* writes about how this situation has arisen:

> There is an epidemic of self-absorption in our society. This epidemic is not rooted in something bad but in something good. Awareness of individual preferences, making provision to have our own needs met, is good for our health. But the danger of this awareness is preoccupation with self. There are some who say that we've come a long way: now we know how to 'look out for number one'. Others see in the phenomenon the seed of relational alienation in our culture.[5]

How often have you seen magazine articles that give ten steps to happiness and top of the list comes 'put yourself at the top of your "to do" list'! There are whole philosophies and psychological theories about looking after ourselves and our interests and this, unsurprisingly, is not good soil from which to nurture healthy, up-building relationships. These days, even at social occasions it is rare to find someone with a grasp of the art of conversation. We're not very good at showing a genuine interest in other people. We'd prefer it if others asked us about ourselves – and then we're on to a topic we *are* interested in! Paul's comment about Timothy in his letter to the Philippians show that this is not a recent phenomenon: 'I have no-one else like him, who takes a genuine interest in your welfare. For everyone looks out for his own interests, not those of Jesus Christ' (Phil. 2:20–21).

Selfless service

We are going to take a short look at Paul's first letter to the Thessalonians. It is an amazing model of selfless service of others by Paul, Silas and Timothy, motivated by love and by the gospel of Christ. Paul says to the church there, 'We loved you so much that we were delighted to share with you not only the gospel of God but our lives as well, because you had become so dear to us' (1 Thess. 2:8). Paul, Silas and Timothy had only stayed with the Thessalonians for two to three weeks, and yet a large number of Jews and Gentiles had been persuaded to put their trust in Christ as Paul reasoned with them from the Scriptures (Acts 17:1–4). In that short time, they must have developed some really strong bonds with the converts and grown to love them deeply. In his first letter to them, we see Paul's pastoral heart and intense interest in the spiritual well-being of the Thessalonians. He writes to them as a pastor, mother and father. He teaches and admonishes them, begs them to stand firm and prays for them constantly, urgently and personally (1 Thess. 2:7,11).

Paul and his co-workers apparently lived utterly transparent lives while they were staying in Thessalonica – they shared their lives with the new converts (1 Thess. 2:8). This means they shared not just the gospel message in words with the people, but modelled it in the way they lived among them. They would have been vulnerable with the new believers there and talked about their struggles and joys in following Christ. This is very important in one-to-one work, since much of the Christian life is 'caught' rather than simply taught. Our one-to-one partner should feel they are getting to know the 'real us' as we share some of what has made us who we are, and some of what we are currently facing in our lives and how we are coping with it as a Christian. In this way, through our friendship, we will be modelling what it means to persevere in the gospel and to strive to live for God in every area of our lives. Paul says to the Thessalonians, 'You are witnesses, and so is God, of how holy, righteous and blameless we were among you who believed' (1 Thess. 2:10).

Furthermore, Paul and his co-workers obviously cared a great deal about the struggles, frustrations and fears of the new believers in Thessalonica; Paul said they were 'gentle among [them], like a mother caring for her little children'. He also talks about 'encouraging, comforting and urging [them] to live *lives* worthy of God' in the same way that a father deals with his own children. These men of the gospel had an urgent, parent-like concern for the welfare and spiritual growth of these baby Christians in Thessalonica. They laboured and prayed for their good and were filled with such joy when they saw these believers standing firm in the face of suffering and living wholly for God (1 Thess.1:6–10; 2:13–14, 19–20a).

It is worth quoting, again, the verses from chapter 3 of 1 Thessalonians, where we see the absolute commitment of these men to the spiritual well-being of the new Christians:

> Therefore, brothers, in all our distress and persecution we were encouraged about you because of your faith. For now we really live, since you are standing firm in the Lord. How can we thank God enough for you in return for all the joy we have in the presence of our God because of you? Night and day we pray most earnestly that we may see you again and supply what is lacking in your faith (1 Thess 3: 7-10).

Caring as a mother

One of the most memorable Christian training talks I have heard was from 1 Thessalonians 2.

> We were being encouraged to think about what 'doing a good job' means in Christian work. One aspect of this was to care for our group members as a mother would her little children (1 Thess. 2:7). Five years on I am a mother of two small children and I *now* realize the poverty of my understanding *then* of what it means to care like a mother. When you have nursed sick children through your own sleep deprivation, dealt with their tantrums, answered endless streams of questions (somewhat) patiently... then you begin to understand what Paul means by caring like a mother!

Now this is a challenging model for caring friendship. What will it mean for us in practice? We can delight to share our lives as well as the gospel with those who are hungry to learn and grow. We can be committed to them as they struggle with applying God's truth to every area of their lives. We can support them if they face persecution from family or friends. We can phone, email, or write to them when we haven't seen them for a while, or simply to give them a word of encouragement. We can do all we can to urge them on to live lives worthy of the gospel.

All of this will need to be done through sharing God's word with them and depending on

God, in prayer, to work in their lives. It will also mean, as we have already seen, 'sharing our lives' with them – getting to know each other more broadly than just 'spiritually'. If our times of one-to-one Bible study and prayer are to have the fullest possible impact on both of our lives, then we need to share something of who we are, what commitments and relationships we have, how we use our time and money, and what struggles we are both facing.

We should learn something of our partner's family and educational background, something of what makes them tick. We should find out about their present living situation and how they are finding it. If they have a hobby, what is it? Singing, sport, cinema, dancing, reading, walking? Perhaps we can have a go with them some time, or go along and watch them in action. And all this should be reciprocal: how can we involve them in our everyday lives wherever possible?

Experiencing life-sharing outside study time

When I was at university, an older guy from my church used to meet up with me to study the Bible and pray together. Each term we went for a drink in a pub outside town to get away from it all. They were good times of

> chatting about nothing in particular, but also a good chance to take spiritual stock of the term; highlights and lowlights. It was a nice change but I sensed that it was part of the reading one-to-one scheme; just part of what one did. They had to do that because that is how you read with someone.
>
> So I remember particularly when we went for a lengthy bike ride one afternoon. That was quality extended time – the 'above and beyond the call of duty' sharing of life, when there were lots of other people he could have spent time with on a precious, summer-term Saturday.
>
> I think we both had 'relationship' issues at the time, and I remember being quite taken aback at how he was finding it all. He shared more than I did which was a real example of humility and normality. In one sense it didn't feel quite right – me being younger – but it was the sort of afternoon that deepened the friendship hugely and I considered it a great honour that he talked as he did.

Genuine Christian friendship *also* means meeting practical needs to the extent we are able. Is there a homesick student who needs a home-cooked meal on a comfy sofa for an evening? Is there a group member who needs somewhere to stay for a few days while they are in between accommodation? Is there a harassed mother who needs an afternoon away from her kids? Is there someone from our group on a summer 'camp' who isn't able to get good Bible teaching, for some reason, that we could send sermon tapes to regularly? Is there someone who is incredibly lonely after the break-up of a long-term relationship and in need of a shoulder to cry on or to be taken out to the cinema (not to see a slushy romance!)?

This is the sort of friendship that should surround one-to-one work. It is this sort of genuine love and concern that should form the foundation to meeting up with someone to share the gospel with them. It is costly in terms of time, emotional energy, vulnerability and sometimes finances. But it is very rewarding. As you see individuals grow in their love for God and others, and as they become more deeply rooted in Christ, you will soon discover why Paul says, 'For what is our hope, our joy, or the crown in which we will glory in the presence of our Lord Jesus Christ when he comes? Is it not you? Indeed you are our glory and joy' (1 Thess. 2:19–20a).

So how can we love like this? The only way is to ask God for it! We need to meditate on Christ's love for us shown in his death on the cross and pray for help to respond to his amazing love for us by loving others in this way – 'We love because he first loved us' (1 Jn. 4:19). The Holy Spirit has poured God's love into our hearts (Rom. 5:5) and he can enable us to share this love with others.

The fruit of sharing your life and the gospel with another

I became a Christian in December 1998. Within a week I had been signed up to a Bible study group, and within a month I had been asked whether I wanted to study the Bible one-to-one with a woman a couple of years older (and significantly wiser!) than me at church. Looking back, these were the best things that could have happened to me, for they brought me into encouraging relationships with other Christians and rooted and grounded me in God's word. However, at the time, I was far from keen to study the Bible one to one with someone – especially with a stranger. Reluctantly though, I agreed.

It felt quite odd during the first few sessions to talk about my life and the Bible with her, but neither of us is exactly shy, and we quickly became close friends. I began to value her as a friend and trust her advice and opinions and to look forward to the times we could meet up. She encouraged me to read the Bible for myself, to start talking to God regularly in prayer, and gently corrected my mistakes when I went off track during our studies. We discovered many riches and treasures in God's word together.

I didn't understand at the time what motivated her, but I was touched nonetheless that she wanted to meet up and how she made time for me, even beyond the study. She looked out for me on Sunday evenings at church and often invited me round to her house for lunch or supper. Moreover, life was very hard that year. I was going out with a non-Christian boyfriend, and found it tough-going as the Spirit tugged me in one direction, while my sinful nature tugged me in another. My grandmother died, my parents hated the fact I had become a Christian and a group of people in my halls of residence were giving me a hard time for my newfound faith. In the midst of the mess, she was emotionally and prayerfully committed to me and always ready to listen.

I had come from a totally non-Christian family, and as such had no female Christian role model. She really laid down her life for me and loved me. She was fantastic because she strove in all her actions and words to point me to the Lord Jesus Christ. I will never forget her love, and always be grateful for it.

Study guide

- How is a focus on prayer consistent with a good understanding of the aims of one-to-one ministry? Use some Bible verses to back up your answer.
- 'We can't all be like Paul' is a statement often heard in Christian circles. To what extent is that *not* true with regard to prayer?
- The Bible is under attack. How would you defend its authority as a source of wisdom and truth today?
- How has your understanding of Christian friendship been enlarged from this chapter? What can we learn about friendship from Christ's statements in John 15:13–15?

Something to do: Ask Christian friends or your small group to tell you what they would most value in a good, faithful older Christian friend. What can you do to be like this to your one-to-one partner?

4

Meeting Regularly to Study the Bible: Before You Meet

1. Setting up the meetings

'How do I actually approach someone about meeting up one-to-one?' This seems to be one of the big fears. Presuming you've picked someone because you already know them and/or they seem really hungry to learn and grow, then they are likely to be excited at the prospect of meeting regularly. Maybe try saying something like, 'I was wondering whether you might like to meet up with me and study the Bible and pray together? I know a number of people [in the church/CU] who do meet up one-to-one together in this way and find it really helpful for their walk with God.'

If you want to initiate one-to-ones with a younger Christian whom you don't know very well, then maybe suggest meeting up for a coffee or having them around for a meal to find out how they are doing and get to know one another better. Meeting up this way a couple of times is a good opportunity to find out how they became a Christian and what their background is, and to discover pressing issues in their Christian life. It is in this context of a growing friendship that you can then suggest meeting up regularly to look at the Bible and pray together, explaining the purpose and aims of a one-to-one friendship to see if it is something they would be interested in.

Where to start with people we don't know well

After starting several one-to-one Bible reading relationships I learned the importance of never assuming anything about a person's standing before Christ. I have met with believers who didn't realize they were secure in their relationship with God and unbelievers who didn't realize they had never turned in repentance to Christ. In the first meeting I now always ask questions like: 'How did your relationship with God begin?' Or 'How would you summarize the Christian message?' Many details are revealed through asking these questions that then help with planning what Bible study is needed for the subsequent meetings.

It can be helpful to get one of the church leaders to set up one-to-one meetings with another church member for you. Those in leadership will often have an eye for those who would greatly benefit from one-to-one discipleship and so can arrange for a more mature Christian to meet up with them.

The issue you then need to tackle with your prospective one-to-one partner is what the arrangement will look like in practice and what commitment is required on their part. It is imperative that you do discuss these questions at this stage in the relationship so that you both have the right expectations.

A note on meeting with a married person

If you set up one-to-one meetings with someone who is married it is worth thinking about how their spouse feels about the arrangement, especially if they aren't Christian. A husband or wife could feel very threatened by this new, close friendship that their spouse has entered into and may be concerned about confidentiality or feeling 'left behind' in their own Christian growth. It is important, therefore, to talk about this issue with your one-to-one partner and encourage them to talk it through with their spouse to check that they are happy with the purpose, parameters and timing of the one-to-one meetings.

How frequently to meet

What is involved in the commitment will depend on the nature of the relationship that already exists between you and on both your and their personal circumstances. If possible, meeting weekly or fortnightly is best, so that you have continuity and momentum in your Bible study and prayer together. If too much time elapses between each meeting, you are more likely to forget what you learnt the last time and what you both prayed for, and there is more possibility of forgetting the next meeting time all together.

How long to go on meeting for

As a very general guide, agreeing to meet up initially for a term or six months is usually a good time span but with the option of 'reviewing it' at the end of that period. Again, as a very general guide, it can be sensible not to commit to any more than one or two years overall. Most of the 'dangers' of one-to-one work noted in chapter 2 are associated with one person having a lot of influence over another. This influence should be temporary so that the younger believer doesn't become dependent on their discipler but on Jesus and on the rest of the church family in healthy interdependence. In addition, since the aim of the meetings is to send them out into the church equipped to stand firm and serve, then it is important to release them as soon as they are ready to do just that.

What to study

Your initial meeting should help you gauge what encouragement and teaching they need and therefore what would be best for you both to study together. You may like to ask them if they have any particular preference over what to study, but be careful – how would you feel about studying Leviticus, Revelation or Haggai together?! You might have the experience, confidence and time to be able to tackle such books for the first time with them, but for many of us, this would be highly intimidating. It may be best to give them a choice of topics that you have experience with and that you think are appropriate for them.

The main options for regular study together include:

- studying a book of the Bible directly (without a study guide)
- studying a Christian theme using different Bible passages but no guide
- studying a Bible book or theme with a study guide
- or studying a Christian book written about a Bible theme (e.g. prayer).

The resources given in chapter 8 should provide some help in this area of what to study. If you are meeting with a more mature Christian, mainly to train them for teaching ministry, you could use the time to do some training in evangelism, leading Bible studies, or giving talks (see point 4 on Training in the chapter 5).

A caveat at this stage, however: studying the Bible directly should be the norm. Studying Bible themes without spending proper time looking at specific passages makes it easier to inadvertently impose our own hobbyhorses rather than searching the Scriptures. And it is best to study a Christian book together only if it gives you opportunities to go back to the Bible together.

Furthermore, although there are many good Bible study aids available, it is preferable for the development of your own Bible-handling skills to prepare Bible studies yourself. In turn, this may prompt your one-to-one partner to work harder at the text himself or herself and grow in their own Bible study skills and understanding. Preparing your own Bible studies can be a very intimidating process at first, but like all things, we grow in confidence as we grow in experience. However, if the thought of it fills you with horror and leads you to abandon the idea of doing one-to-one, then don't panic. We're all at different starting points and there is great freedom in how to use these one-to-one times, so long as God's truth is central to the meeting. We should feel free to use one of the helps mentioned above – and maybe over time you can suggest to your one-to-one partner that you both have a go at preparing your own studies and give each other feedback on them.

For a non-Christian, studying a gospel account of Jesus is the best way to introduce them to Christianity. Mark's Gospel is a great place to start since it is the shortest of the four (see chapter 8 for two sample studies in Mark). It also has a fantastic opening sentence to focus the reader on what the message of Christianity is all about: 'The beginning of the gospel [good news] about Jesus Christ, the Son of God' (Mk. 1:1). For Christians still struggling with the identity and mission of Jesus Christ, again, Mark is probably the best book to study. For a Christian who is clearer on Jesus, but needs pushing on how to grow in the gospel then one of the shorter letters to the early churches, such as Colossians (see chapter 8 for two sample studies) or 1 Peter, can be a great place to start. Having said that, it can be helpful with a young Christian whom you don't know very well to do a short course on gospel basics to check the foundations of their faith, before you go on to study a particular book. There are a number of possible resources given in chapter 8 but an eight-week course on the following topics and passages could be used:

1. Right with God (Rom. 3:21–26)
2. Trusting in God (Eph. 2:1–10)
3. Life in the Spirit (Rom. 8:5–17)
4. Listening to God (2 Tim. 3:10–17)
5. Talking to God (Phil. 4:4–7)
6. Meeting with God's family (Eph. 4:1–6)
7. Reaching the world (Col. 4:2–6)
8. Keeping going to the end (Heb.12:1–11)

For those we may be specifically trying to train to teach others, studying 2 Timothy or Titus would be a good plan (for more on training see chapter 5), as these were written to (young) church leaders.

2. Bible study preparation

The idea of preparing and writing your own Bible study may seem a bit daunting at first. It is tempting just to stick to pre-prepared published material written by the 'experts'. And in some ways there's nothing wrong with that. God has given us different gifts within the body of his church (1 Cor. 12) and to some he has given the gift of teaching the Bible. Many of the resources listed in chapter 8 have been produced by people with that gift, and there is no shame in using them.

We need to make sure, however, that those teachers (with the Bible study materials that they produce) don't become like 'priests' who stand between us and God and tell us what God is saying. We need to avoid the situation where we feel that we don't have access to what God is saying on our own, but have to go via the priest – the Bible then belongs to the academics, or the insightful teachers. We can all understand the Bible for ourselves, to some extent. This has been called the *perspicuity* of the Bible – the Bible is clear and understandable. We can see this in the fact that the epistles were written to whole congregations and the gospels (especially John) were written to a wide audience. The point is, the Bible is God's book, and with God's Spirit we can understand it. All it will take on our part is a humble and prayerful heart, and a bit of hard work. This section contains some basic guidelines that will help you do the groundwork for writing your own Bible study from scratch.

What you will need:

- A good Bible translation, such as the New International Version or the more recent English Standard Version (make sure the person you are meeting up with has the same version). However, having two or three different versions of the text will help in your preparation – for example, the NIV, the ESV and the NASB. You can download a number of different translations from {www.gospel-com.net} – just click on the 'Biblegateway' button and type in the passage you want.

- Reference materials where appropriate (Bible dictionary, commentaries, maps, etc.).
- Time! You will probably need between thirty minutes and two hours to prepare a study, depending on your experience, knowledge of the text, length of passage and so on.

The aim of studying a passage

We need to be 'work[men] who [do] not need to be ashamed and who correctly handle the word of truth' (2 Tim. 2:15). This means working at the text to discover what God is saying, first of all to the original hearers, and then to us through his message to them. So we need to ask of each passage, 'What is God's big message in this section?' Scripture is written logically in sentences and paragraphs and not in sound bites. We need to study the text to get to the heart of it and work out what the big points are before we can see how it should be applied to our lives. When we learn lots of new truths from a passage, we need always to be asking, 'But *why* is the author telling us these things?' This helps us to be challenged by the passage at a deeper level than 'a list of two things I learnt about Jesus and three things I have to change'. The deeper level of challenge is that of having our whole perspective and values addressed, so that then we make changes to our lives out of the right motives (faith), and not just through duty or fear of people or trying to earn God's favour.

The three key steps of Bible study

A. Observation

In this first step we discover **what the passage *says***. This requires more than a casual reading of the passage. We need to learn how to sift through the words of the passage in order to discover what the writer is saying, which may not be what you expect it to say, or what you thought it said on a superficial reading. Bible dictionaries and maps may be helpful (though not essential) when it comes to unusual words, ideas or unfamiliar place names and locations. Sometimes it helps to break the passage into smaller sections and look for how they fit together – perhaps even try giving each section a title. Keep your eye out for clues that the author might have left to direct us to the big point he is making, e.g. repeated words or ideas, summary statements, etc.

B. Interpretation

Here, we will discover **what the passage *means***. We need to discover the God-given meaning of the passage through asking right interpretative questions. It is imperative that we discover the correct interpretation, for if we get that wrong, our application will be wrong too. The key tool for this step is *context*. Good questions to ask to get at the various levels of context are:

- What is said immediately before/after this verse?
- What is said before/after this passage?
- What is the flow of the author's argument?
- What point(s) would we miss if we didn't have this passage?
- How does this book fit in with the Bible story?

A good thing to aim for in working out the meaning of the passage is a 'theme sentence' or short sentence that captures the main point. This prevents us from taking away six unrelated truths from the passage without thinking about how they fit together, and it focuses on the one big thing the author is saying.

C. Application

Finally, we will discover **what the passage *means to us***. The Bible was not given merely to inform us about God and his plans, but to transform our lives! We need to learn how to apply the passage in practical ways to our lives. But we mustn't do this too quickly. In one sense the Bible was not written directly to us, but to people long ago in history, such as 'the saints in

Philippi' or the Jews in exile in Babylon. To apply the passage correctly we need first to ask what it meant to the original hearers in their context, before working out the universal truth that transcends culture and time and applies to our situation.

The application of any given truth of God's word basically falls into one or more of the following categories:

- *Belief* – a growth or change in my understanding and knowledge of God, Jesus, the gospel, or a deepening trust in God's promises.
- *Attitude* – a change in my heart to do with what I think about people or things or life.
- *Behaviour* – a change in what I actually say and do.

3. Writing the study

It might sound obvious, but the aim of any Bible study should be to teach the theme and aim of the passage being studied! It is possible to do all the preparation on the text for nothing if the study ends up getting hijacked by a red herring and the big points are entirely missed.

If you are studying a book of the Bible together it is best to do your first study as an introduction to or summary of the book. This involves both of you reading and rereading the book all the way through before you meet and then discussing the recurring themes, tone, main sections, and big ideas of the book. This will give you a clearer framework from within which to work as the weeks go on. You may, however, want to come back to your summary at the end of the book and see if there are any conclusions you want to modify. A sample of this type of study for Colossians is given in chapter 8.

Questions

You will need to ask questions that open up the meaning of the passage you are studying. Many people experienced in leading Bible studies don't prepare questions in advance for their one-to-one times. They prefer the flexibility of working through a passage in a more relaxed way. However, rarely will this approach yield success in the hands of someone inexperienced in leading Bible studies! It is much safer to have at least a few prepared questions to help provide some structure and direction, to have anticipated any difficult bits and to have worked out what points to spend most time discussing together.

The best thing is to use the same types of questions as you used in your own preparation:

- *Observation*: What? Who? When? These are questions that will get someone to be clear on what the passage actually says. Try to be imaginative with these if at all possible. For example, one idea for getting the main facts and background details of a passage might be to ask, 'If this was a film, what would the main scenes be? Where would the camera be pointing? What kind of background music would you need?' etc.
- *Interpretation*: Why? How? These are questions to draw out the *significance* of the points: What does it all mean? What is the big point that the author is making?
- *Application*: So what? These questions draw out the eternal truth from the big point and then provoke discussion on how we should be responding to it.

Good questions will:

- make them look hard at the passage, so they can't answer simply from their own Christian experience, e.g. 'Looking at verses 1–6, what do we learn about ...?' (see box entitled 'Get them to answer from the Bible' in chapter 5);
- be simple and understandable on first hearing (not too many long clauses); this may mean giving them a statement first, followed by a short question;

- require some thought, i.e. they certainly need more than a yes/no answer;
- lead them to the main point of the passage – not away from it on a tangent.

During the study, you will also want to make use of supplementary questions:

- to check their understanding, 'What do you mean by that?' 'How did you reach that answer?';
- to turn them back to the text such as, 'How does what you've said fit with verse 6?', 'How do verses 12–14 introduce the idea for us?', Or simply, 'Look at what the text actually says!';
- to push them further on a point such as, 'Go on' or, 'Push that idea further!';
- to anticipate misunderstandings or red herrings.

Finally, summaries are very helpful and should be used fairly frequently:

- You can get *them* to summarize to confirm their understanding.
- Or *you* can summarize to make sure they go away with a clear point if you've had a slightly confused discussion.
- You can use summaries to draw a line under a point so you can move on to the next one.

- Always give a summary towards the end of the study, before the main application, to ensure that you are applying the right point!

Remember: your material should be person-centred not programme-centred. Have your particular one-to-one partner in mind as you write your questions and if you use the material again with someone else, go over and check your study to see if it's pitched at the right level for the new person.

NB It might sound very obvious, but it is still worth stressing that prayer should be an activity that starts, finishes and infuses all our Bible study. We must never treat studying the Bible as a merely academic exercise. As Christians we should always pray for God's help to understand his word and for hearts and minds to accept the challenge it brings to us and for strength to put it into practice. We should also pray for help in actually writing good questions and teaching God's word clearly, faithfully and passionately.

Study guide

- Work out what ninety-minute time slots you would have available in your week in which you could meet regularly with someone for one-to-one.

- Why is it better to end up preparing Bible studies yourself rather than just using other people's material?

Something to do: Prepare an introductory study on Colossians 1:15–23 and ask an older Christian to have a look at it and give you feedback.

5

Meeting Regularly to Study the Bible: When You Meet

1. The practicalities

As we have seen already, studying the Bible one-to-one means more than just studying the Bible together. When you meet, you will want to get to know each other better and find out what's been happening in each other's lives. It is also helpful to cover certain issues over time – theological ones and lifestyle ones, to make sure that core Christian doctrines are understood and that they are being lived out appropriately (see section 3 below).

There are no hard-and-fast rules as to how you use the time – whatever suits you both – but this chapter contains a few suggestions. There's a tendency for the Bible study time to get shorter and shorter over the weeks and for 'chat time' to take over. It is good to remember, if this happens, that it's the Bible that is the power of God for change (see chapter 3, section 2 on the Bible). It is best to use the time you have available as strategically as possible for their Christian lives and ministry and to open God's word with them as much as possible.

One-to-one meetings can take anything between twenty minutes and two hours depending on the time available, on personality and gender. As a general rule, women may need slightly longer than men. From interviews and questionnaires, a number of men have commented that it is perfectly possible for them to have a productive time of Bible study with another man in around fifteen to twenty minutes, whereas there were no such comments from the women! The most common length of time to meet for a Bible study, chat and prayer is between one and one-and-a-half hours. Such a meeting might take the form of: catch-up chat (as kettle boils!)–study–pray–chat. The proportion of time spent chatting informally and spent studying the Bible will vary depending on the length of your meeting, the situation of the individual and on how much Bible input they are already getting in the rest of their life.

Just a note of caution about *where* you meet – do try to get somewhere quiet, where you are not going to be disturbed and where you can pray. It is always good to have some drinks and snacks to enjoy while studying! It can be best to meet on your own territory, not theirs, so that you can deal with distractions without any embarrassment still you may have to make it clear from the start of the meeting when you need to be finished by, so that you both know when you need to wrap things up. Having said all that, it is better to meet anywhere than not to meet at all (see below)!

Starbucks as a one-to-one venue

When I was working in London, I was keen to meet up with another woman to read the Bible and pray before work. The problem was that we couldn't find anywhere to meet, so we ended up doing Bible studies in Starbucks. It wasn't ideal as it could be crowded and there was music playing, but we decided that it was better than not meeting up. We soon got used to shutting out the noise and not worrying about what people were thinking as we had our Bibles open – a great lesson in being unashamed of being Christian!

2. Leading the study

Setting the right tone

The tone of the study time needs to be relaxed and informal. Your time together should be exciting and a joy as you study God's word together. This doesn't always mean it will be fun or easy or even light-hearted, but that it should never become a burden to be dreaded – a time when they feel 'under the spotlight' and nervous. This relaxed atmosphere will come from confidence that God will work through our weakest efforts at pointing people to Jesus and from a humility that recognizes that you are just fellow Christians meeting together for mutual encouragement and growth. Confidence can also be improved with good preparation, so that you have a certain degree of clarity about the passage and have worked at writing some good discussion questions.

However, we need to be flexible when we meet together. If your one-to-one partner arrives and announces that they have had a traumatic confrontation with a friend or colleague, or that their mother has been diagnosed with cancer, then it might not be appropriate to plough on ahead with our prepared Bible study. There are times when we need simply to sit and listen, to console, comfort and encourage. We will talk more about this in the next two chapters.

Responding to answers

As you start the study, simply ask your good questions *once* and wait! The temptation is always to rephrase too quickly, or even to start answering your own question. A good question will make them think, so there should be a small period of silence while the old grey cells are at work! Also, be sure to listen to their answer. Don't be so focused on your next question that you ignore what they say. Respond to their answers using supplementary questions to push them further or to clarify their understanding. If they are wrestling well with the text, be enthusiastic. As you go further in your study times, it is good to start pushing them – say, 'Go on!' 'Do explain.' 'What do you mean?'

Remember, though, what was said in chapter 2 about the freedom to be who we are in all Christian ministry. God has made us all unique and there is no set 'style' for looking at God's word with another individual. Ask questions in a way that you feel comfortable with and go at a pace you can both cope with.

Get them to answer from the Bible

I once started meeting up to study the Bible with a slightly cocky, first-year student. We read the passage together, and then I asked my first question, at which point he closed his Bible, put it on the table in front of him, and then started to answer the question – answering I guess from his own thoughts and ideas – which were hopeless! I waited for him to finish, then said that actually he might find some help in the passage we had just read – perhaps in verse 4? So he opened his Bible again, and reading verse 4, saw the answer straightaway and told me. But then he closed his Bible and put it down again. I decided I had better explain we were trying to find out what God thought – and that meant reading the Bible.

How different from another incident some years later. Not a one to one, but a Bible study group this time. I took some cups of tea to some women doing a Bible study with my wife. As I went into the room they had just started the study and I heard my wife ask a question. As she asked the question, all their heads dropped in unison to look at the part of the Bible they had just read. No one spoke immediately – they were looking for the answer in the passage.

When I reflected on it, I remembered that all those women had no past history of Christianity – so they really didn't know anything. The good thing about that was that when you asked them a question, they never answered from ideas they already had – because they didn't have any! They had to look at the Bible, and so filled their minds with what God was saying.

What about dealing with 'red herrings'– those questions that take you way off the text you are studying and into a whole new area of discussion? There should be great freedom in one-to-ones to tackle issues that are raised from the passage but aren't necessarily *in* the passage. Tthat is one of the advantages of one-to-one studies over group studies or sermons and is a great opportunity to expand and deepen our understanding of many Christian doctrines and application issues. However, it is worth giving a word of warning at this stage about these 'red herrings'. Although it is helpful to tackle their questions or issues on occasion, it is not helpful to do this every time you meet. If you do go off down these side alleys every time:

- you will lose continuity, and your sense of context, structure and flow if studying a book;
- you may be indulging a proud desire to pin every bit of God's truth down immediately;
- you may be dealing with felt needs rather than letting the Bible set God's agenda;
- you will rarely get to good application and so you may never be working through the implications of God's truth for your lives.

It is important, therefore, to ensure that the subject or text you are meant to be studying is the focus of your discussion together, while at the same time allowing time to cover other areas of Christian doctrine and issues of lifestyle and service (see section 3 below).

Memorizing Scripture together can be a fruitful way to end a study from time to time. For example, you can pick a key verse from the passage and have a go at saying it together with your Bibles closed and perhaps offer to test each other next time you meet. The Navigators' Topical Memory System (NIV, NASB, AV, NKJV; Nav Press, 1986, USA) can be a very useful tool for this.

Enjoying it

David Fletcher has been in ordained Christian ministry for many years, several of them as rector of St Ebbe's Church in Oxford. He comments that the phrase 'chocolate box approach to Bible study' is generally used pejoratively or as a criticism to reading the Bible without certain checks of structure, context and so on. 'I am fully aware that this can be a very dangerous practice and that the Bible needs to be handled correctly with due attention given to the context of each verse. However, I do feel that with this great diligence in handling the Bible correctly we can lose something of the wonder of God's word. Reading the Bible with someone should feel like enjoying a large piece of chocolate cake together! The truths should be savoured and enjoyed not analysed to their death. The activity should be a joy not an academic task.'

Praying together

As you draw the study to a close, try to pray through the big applications of the passage and where appropriate, pray the truth through for specific circumstances in your lives. In fact, where specific application is proving to be a struggle in your studies, sharing prayer requests can be a real help to applying what you have learnt to both your particular circumstances. A helpful way of combining application and prayer is simply to ask, 'Is there anything that has particularly struck you from this passage that we can pray about?' Many people find that it is helpful to have a time of praying through what they have learned together and then a separate time of praying for other things that have arisen over the week.

If the person is very shy about praying out loud at first, then don't wait for ever for them in awkward silence! It might be better to ask them if they feel able to pray aloud and encourage them by saying, 'Why don't you pray a short prayer about those things first, so I don't steal your thoughts before you come to pray!' We shouldn't pressurize them to pray if they are unwilling, but some gentle encouragement to 'give it a go' after a few weeks will really help them in the long run. Simply remind them that they are praying to God and he doesn't mind one bit if we stumble or repeat things or forget what we were going to say! They might prefer to write down a short prayer and then pray from what they have written. Confidence in corporate prayer simply comes through practice.

Before you leave

Make sure you give them the next passage to read and think about in advance of the following meeting, as well as prep questions if appropriate (see box below). It is also a good idea to check that the normal time and place are still suitable for your next meeting.

Prep questions

When I met up to read with someone I had tended not to give them much prep for our sessions because I didn't want to burden them. Recently, however, this has changed somewhat.

I was given a copy of some Bible studies on Christian basics that I decided to try out with a new Christian I was starting to meet with. The study booklet came with a number of observation, meaning and application questions on the passage for each week. The plan was that both of us would work through these questions before we met and then discuss them when we met up.

I was initially rather nervous about giving a young Christian this work to do as prep and reassured her that there was no pressure whatsoever and to just do what she felt like. But week-by-week, I was amazed at the time she put into studying the passage – at times she did much more thinking about the passage than I did in advance of meeting up! I think she just enjoyed looking at the Bible for herself and it meant that our study time was a joy with much more opportunity to tackle her questions on tricky issues the passage had raised and time for application and prayer.

I am aware that Becky is a student who is used to doing such study and possibly has more time than workers or mums, but it has convinced me to at least give people the option of preparing with questions before the study so that we can both get more out of the time we meet together.

Rico Tice's advice on meeting one-to-one with non-Christians

The main thing you need is the courage to get the Bible open. And please remember that the first five minutes with the Bible open are the worst. They will feel a bit embarrassed because this is new, so just get the passage open and teach it. Very quickly you'll both be lost in the study. I have the following advice:

1. Grab the opportunity
I don't ask people to read the Bible with me out of the blue. It will follow a guest service or a 'Christians in Sport' day or a conversation in which I have sensed there is some spiritual hunger. And sometimes I'll ring and say, 'Look, it was great to have you on that "Christians in Sport" golf day. Would you like to follow it up a bit by meeting and looking at a passage in the Bible, which I think is appropriate?' I emphasize the fact that it's personal by saying, 'It would be great to just have some time together, where other people aren't torpedoing us with their agendas.'

I will often meet them in a public place for a coffee or a drink and I may well have photocopied the passage we look at so that they don't feel embarrassed that people can see us reading the Bible. It also enables them to take the passage away with them.

2. Get them talking
I start the study with an open question. Often, particularly with guys, they are embarrassed to speak because they have so little knowledge of the subject, so I'll start with an open question that makes them feel they are contributing. Invariably I go to Mark 1 verse 1 and, having read the verse, 'The beginning of the gospel about Jesus Christ, the Son of God', I'll start with the question: 'What is your experience of religion?' and 'What is the experience of your contemporaries and the culture?' After they've talked about the stereotypes, I will then say, 'Can you see what Mark's experience of the Christian faith is? It's great news (gospel) about Jesus Christ, the Son of God – so it's about a person, it's about a relationship, and if that isn't your primary experience of the Christian faith, you've been misled.' That open question gets them talking and then leads us into the passage.

3. Get them into the passage
With Mark chapter 1 I'll then say, 'I think there are seven witnesses as to who Jesus is – to his identity – in the first 20 verses. Who are they?' So that one question makes them work

their way through the passage. Again, I'm so often looking for one question, which reveals the big idea of the passage.

4. Get personal and passionate

It is so important, particularly with non-Christians, to show how the passage has affected your own life, so not only are you exploring (listening to where they are at) and explaining (teaching the truth), you are also encouraging by showing how it's real for you.

I'll often show what from Psalm 103, verses 14 to 17. Having asked the question, 'What does this passage say about humans and what does it say about God?' I will then apply the realization that we are dust and that we do flourish like a flower of the field, but then its place remembers it no more, by speaking of the effect my godfather's sudden death had on me. So I'll say, 'When I realized verse 17, that from everlasting to everlasting the Lord's love is with those who fear him, it made me see that I had to invest in the one who could guarantee eternity. That was obvious once I realized we are just grass.'

5. Get a best thought

I will often keep the study time short, say no more than fifteen minutes and maybe only five minutes, but I do want to know what struck them most, not least because it will help me to explore where they are at in their understanding and, therefore, know what to teach them next time.

6. Tackle the heart of the matter

If an issue to do with lifestyle or morals comes up as we study, I will always try and turn it back to the heart of the matter – our desire to be in control of our lives. So if they ask, 'Do you think it's wrong for me to be sleeping with my girlfriend?' I might answer, 'God is primarily concerned about us living in right relationship with him. Let's work out what it means to be in relationship with God and who God is and then we can work out whether we can trust him or not.'

7. Get another date in the diary

It's great to say, 'Well, do you want to pop another date in to meet?' and then put that date in the diary, so that a routine can be established. I then will maybe pray, particularly if a major issue of concern to them has arisen. I'll often try and do it with the Bible passage as a basis, so for example, 'Thank you, Lord God, that the Christian faith is great news about Jesus. Please help us to understand what this means.' So we pray about what God has spoken to us about.

3. Other issues to address

We have mentioned the need to strike a balance between going off on tangents and keeping the allocated text as the focus of your study. But while aiming to stick mainly to the passage in your 'study time' of around twenty to sixty minutes, there may be plenty of opportunity to chat before and after your Bible study time and to meet up outside your regular meeting time to get to know each other better and to cover 'other material'. Over the span of the year or so that you meet up in this way, it is a good idea to aim to cover some of the key doctrines and certain lifestyle issues that won't necessarily crop up in the passages you are studying. This is simply a further part of trying to ground them in the gospel, to grow their faith and to encourage them to live it out more thoroughly. This is also an opportunity for you to do some further reading around and battling with these issues yourself! Teaching others about godly Christian living in all areas of our lives can often be a speedy road to repentance for ourselves in the first place. Below are some examples of subjects to talk about:

- **Doctrine** – e.g. assurance, confession, God's sovereignty and predestination,

Jesus' return, the Holy Spirit, faith, biblical manhood and womanhood, spiritual gifts, the Bible, the church, prayer, witness, etc.

- **Lifestyle/service issues** – e.g. evangelism; sex and relationships; family; career and money; Christian service; prayer life; pride, etc. In the box below is a list that some people use for this 'spiritual health check'.

Twelve (possible) Gs to cover in one-to-one work

Gold Attitude to money – giving?
Girls/Guys Sex; pornography; going out with non-Christians
Glory Pride
Grog Getting drunk
Grumbling Moaning on
Gossiping Talking about people behind their back
Government Breaking the law, e.g. cycling without lights, breaking copyright
Gullibility Believing everything you hear at church/Christian Union without asking, 'Is that what the Bible really says?'
Goggle-box Wasting time
Going to bed too late Ruins our chance of spending time with God tomorrow morning, and makes us irritable and useless!

Giving up Failing to persevere
Guilt When you think of the other Gs and forget grace!

We don't have the space here to run through these different doctrines and lifestyle/service issues and what you might like to cover for each one. A number of books on most of these subjects are listed in chapter 8. You could agree to read one of these books together over the space of a month or so and then discuss the issues it raises over a meal, perhaps. One subject worth mentioning specifically is that of 'quiet times' or the devotional time we spend with God each day. There can be so much confusion and often a great sense of burden and guilt in this area and yet it is fundamental to Christian growth and perseverance, at the heart of our relationship with God. This is something that you should definitely talk about together, honestly sharing your frustrations and encouragements, and helping each other to develop a deeper devotional life (see the Appendix).

A note on tackling 'issues' with someone

When we are discussing the lifestyle issues in particular, we need to ensure we have the following attitudes:

1. Allow them to fail

When asking questions about someone's walk with God, make it perfectly clear they don't have to come up with the right answer. We don't want them thinking when we've asked a question, 'What's the right answer? What do they expect me to say?' And when we ask someone, 'I expect you've had a quiet time every day for the last two weeks, haven't you?' it's asking them to impress. It's difficult for them to say, 'No – I haven't actually.' Much better to ask, 'With a job like yours it must be very difficult to find any time to read the Bible at all …'

2. Be in the fight together

We mustn't put ourselves in the situation where people can't ask questions back. We want to encourage them to ask us questions. Remember, it's not a pupil-teacher relationship, or an employer-employee relationship, it's one Christian to another, within the family of God. They need to know that we are in the fight to be godly disciples together and so we must both be applying God's word faithfully and honestly.

3. Speak the truth in love

Truth is vital for a healthy Christian life. We need to keep hearing the truth about God, truth about the world and truth about ourselves. A good friend will always speak the truth to us, even when it is uncomfortable. It may mean a correction or a rebuke, but we live in a culture where to try to correct error or rebuke sin in someone is seen as judgemental. Political correctness rules the day and therefore to challenge someone in this way is unacceptable because it's implying they're wrong. We must resist that thinking – it is not Christian. Proverbs 27:6 tells us, 'Wounds from a friend can be trusted, but an enemy multiplies kisses.' We must correct because we are Christian, but we have no right to do it unless we love them (for more on this see the next chapter).

This is an area where we need to know ourselves. Are we rather trigger-happy or do we feel an almost pathological inability to correct anyone? We also need to know the person we're talking to. Some will just need a hint, while others will need it spelt out in capital letters twenty feet high. Any correction must be done with great humility and with love. Critical words can go very deep into our hearts – we all know that from teachers at school, or parents who criticized us years ago. We need to pick only serious issues of wrong thinking about God or the gospel or those relating to ongoing rebellion in a particular area of their life.

Imagine, for instance, that your one-to-one partner is going out with a non-Christian. What do you do? Love demands that we correct them and we do so early. It is simply not loving to let the relationship develop, 'to wait and see if they're serious' before we say anything, because by that stage it's much harder to end the relationship. So don't be afraid to correct. If it's an issue that you know is a battleground, ask permission, 'Do you mind if I ask you about ... and by the way please ask me about ... because that's my battleground.'

4. Watch our motives

We must always watch out for motives other than love which drive us to correct or rebuke someone. Are we frustrated with someone that they are not growing at the pace we would like? Is their ongoing struggle with a certain issue simply irritating us? Is our pride driving us to speak to them about an issue, because we don't want people to think we're not doing a 'good job' with them one-to-one? All sorts of selfish motives can creep in to one-to-one ministry and we need to acknowledge them and then put them to death and pursue love as a motive.

4. Training

Our vision is to see one-to-one work multiplying. We want to be growing Christians to maturity so they in turn can help other new believers to grow in their faith and so on. This is what Paul is talking about in 2 Timothy 2:2 – 'And the things you have heard me say in the presence of many witnesses entrust to reliable men who will also be qualified to teach others.' If you look carefully, there are four generations of people in this verse, representing a chain of successive gospel workers to whom the baton is passed: Paul, Timothy ('you'), the reliable men, and the others.

This specific training of 'reliable' individuals so that they are equipped to teach others should be a key component in your meeting. But who are these 'reliable men'? It means those who are trustworthy with the gospel – who will handle the word of truth correctly (2:15) and hold to the apostolic teaching, 'with faith and love in Christ Jesus' (1:13). There may be individuals who you suspect have the 'gift of teaching', but putting them 'through the simulator' and getting them to have a go is the only way to prove this.

Passing on the baton

After finishing a fantastic year of one-to-one discipleship with a student worker in my church, where I grew to feel safe, secure and able to grow in my relationship with God, the daunting suggestion that I should now pray and think about someone who I could disciple brought feelings of doubt, panic and disbelief. How could I, still a student myself, with what seemed like little knowledge or experience, possibly even consider discipling someone else? Besides which, what poor unsuspecting student could I find who would ever agree to meet up regularly with me? I smiled and said I'd pray about it!

Over the next few months, as I became involved in Christian Union leadership, I began to see how invaluable the support, teaching and training I had received was to my service within the CU. Furthermore, I recognized how significant personal support and discipleship was in seeing people grow in Christ and reach out to others with the gospel. As I encouraged others in the CU to be involved in accountable relationships, I was well aware that 'to whom much is given, much is expected'. But, more than that, I wanted to be involved in helping someone discover more of God through his word. The big question though, was still 'who?' There really didn't seem to be anyone suitable. Ironically, during the most stressful period of the second-year medical exams, a new girl started coming to CU, a new Christian who wanted to know more and be able to explain what she believed to her suspicious friends.

When the opportunity came I spoke to her, saying it would be great if she and I could spend some time together next year, looking at the basics of Christianity and praying for our friends. Her response was amazing, she was enthusiastic and so grateful that someone was willing to do that with her. She also said that she wasn't very good at praying out loud and would love to have someone to help her learn to pray! Later that night she texted me to thank me again and say that she was really excited about next year now. It was an amazing example of how God provides.

At the back of our minds it might be worth having an outline of Paul's second letter to Timothy, with its focus on ministry training. In this letter, Paul is challenging Timothy to remain true to the apostolic gospel, even if it involves suffering, and to do the hard work of training these 'reliable men' to pass it on to others, so that the gospel spreads and is not lost. Let's have a look at the areas Paul focuses on so that we can learn from them in training others.

Foundations – Paul briefly summarizes the gospel to remind Timothy of the faith they share (2 Tim. 1:8–14). He challenges Timothy to remain faithful to these foundations and not be ashamed of teaching it to others, whatever the personal cost.

Are our one-to-one partners still putting gospel truth at the fore, attending a Bible teaching church, and reading Christian books?

Focus – Paul encourages Timothy to remain focused on:

- service (1:6; 2:1–17; 3:10 – 4:5)
- avoiding bad influences (2:14 – 3:9)
- heaven (1:1; 2:8–13; 4:1,8) and the promise of future glory that makes all the hardship now worth it.

Are our one-to-one partners sharing these priorities?

Friendship – The letter starts and ends with reminders of friendship with Jesus, and is peppered throughout with reminders of Paul's friendship with Timothy (1:3–5 in particular), and with other mutual acquaintances (4:19–21). Each of these names will have had deep meaning to Timothy even if they have little meaning to us.

What priority are our one-to-one partners placing on their devotional lives with Jesus, and their relationships with friends?

These are great questions to ask, but be careful! If any Christian could put ticks against every one of these items he or she would be doing outstandingly well. The reality is that we are all going to be falling short in one or more of these areas, if not all of them – and I am sure Timothy would have been too. Ploughing through a list like this can be at best tiresome, at worst incredibly discouraging, as our one-to-one partners sense they are not making the grade. We must make sure we encourage people with the grace of God and not slip into legalism. But that doesn't take away the very big challenge issued by Paul in his pastoral letters for those involved in church leadership to be living transparently godly lives. We must 'watch [our] life and doctrine closely' (1 Tim. 4:16) and encourage those we are training for teaching ministry to do the same.

Practically

You could train someone by working through this book with them. An easy way of putting them through the simulator is to get them to lead your Bible study in your last few weeks together. You could perhaps start by having one or two sessions on how to handle Scripture correctly and how to write questions for a study. Then you get them to lead a study. You could maybe take turns in leading the last few studies. If it would feel too artificial for you to answer their questions (perhaps because you both know that you know the answers anyway!) then you can ask them what response they would hope to get from their question.

You can then assess whether their question would have achieved that aim. We need to be very encouraging at first, pointing out obvious mistakes like questions with only one-word answers (which are fairly common at first!) or lack of application questions. But then get slightly tougher on the third or fourth time, feeding back on their handling of the passage, the structure of their questions and the degree to which their study would have pushed someone in terms of understanding and application. This way, they will feel far more confident to start studying with someone else, because they have been through the simulator with you and grown through the experience.

It is a good idea to meet up with them from time to time once they have started doing one-to-one with someone else to encourage them and allow them to talk through their experience and any difficulties they are having (and to keep caring for them more generally – see the next two chapters on follow-up).

Evangelism should be a key aspect of your training. You could both practice giving your testimony, and giving each other feedback. Maybe you could arrange for them to give a talk at a school, youth group or other such meeting and go with them. Get them to learn a gospel outline and practice on you, then get them to pray for an opportunity to give it to a non-Christian friend over the coming weeks and talk about how it went (God will usually answer such prayers!). Perhaps you could help them to organize a 'meal with a message' where they join up with another Christian friend or housemate or with their spouse and invite a number of non-Christian friends along with a speaker to give a five-minute gospel presentation (you might be the speaker).

It is definitely worth the effort!

I was quite apprehensive at first about meeting one-to-one with someone. I was worried about a) not knowing the girl very well and her finding it a bit odd that I suggested such a thing! b) not knowing my Bible well enough and not being able to answer her questions, and c) not having enough time to prepare.

Nonetheless I took the plunge and asked her if she wanted to meet up with me. She seemed enthusiastic and we arranged to meet every week in her halls of residence room, setting aside about one hour (although I found that we needed longer than an hour as time went on – it was lovely to chat about all sorts of things as we got to know each other better, and the Bible studies became more in-depth). I need not have worried about anything. Organizing my time to set aside half an hour to prepare the study was such a benefit to me. I learnt so much by going though a book of the Bible and thinking about questions and the answers. As the weeks went by I also learnt which sort of questions really help bring out the meaning and application of a passage as well as helping the person answer from the passage itself rather than general knowledge.

Also, meeting with a fellow female Christian was so encouraging and I found that I learnt from her questions and the points she made. How amazing it was to see someone grow in their knowledge and understanding of Christ and really start to live out what they know. By the end of the year I had a much deeper grasp of Colossians and also knowledge of how to share the book with others. I had made a really close friend, with whom I spent time socially as well as for mutual encouragement. I had grown in confidence in leading Bible studies and answering difficult questions. I have also learnt that, with a bit of organization, I can do more with my time than I realized.

But most of all, meeting with someone one-to-one made me rely on God for his wisdom and strength in a new way, as I knew that without him, I would be totally hopeless at teaching the Bible or making time to do it.

My advice is: If at all hesitant about reading one to one then just get stuck in and God will guide you and teach you through it.

Matthias Media have produced a very helpful seven-week evangelism training course that can be worked through with your one-to-one partner. It uses their Two Ways to Live gospel outline and covers topics such as 'Looking at biblical principles of evangelism' and 'Discussing practical problems associated with evangelism'. The course material can be ordered from The Good Book Company website at www.thegoodbook.co.uk or call 0845 225 0880.

Study guide

- In a sentence, how would you summarize the outcome of a well-constructed Bible study question?
- In your experience of being on the receiving end of Bible study in either a group or one-to-one situation, what do you think are the things that make a good or bad study?
- On page 102, David Fletcher is quoted as saying that reading the Bible should be 'a joy, not an academic task'. How can we make sure our times studying the Bible are like this?

- List all the places you regularly visit or have access to. Which make good venues for one-to-one? If you can't think of any – what about places your friends, family or church have access to?

Something to do: Ask a friend if they would do you a favour by being on the receiving end of your one-to-one study on Colossians 1:15–23 so they can assess your approach. What are their comments at the end of the study?

6

Meeting Occasionally

1. Making conversations count

This chapter will tackle the issue of how to help those whom you don't have the time or opportunity to meet regularly to grow in their understanding of the gospel and its implications for their life. Although much of what is said will apply equally to regular, structured Bible study partnerships, the focus in this chapter will be one-to-one work that is done in more informally scheduled meetings. It may be with someone you are following up from a summer camp or a 'mission' event, or a present cell/home group member, or a past group member, or maybe someone you used to meet up with regularly for one-to-one Bible study, or perhaps an existing contact or even someone new who has just arrived in your church.

It is probably fair to say that these times of 'quality catch-up' are the lifeblood of a well-functioning church, where individual members are taking seriously the command to 'love one another' by taking time out for other members of the church family. If Christians don't have a vision for this sort of occasional meeting to encourage one another, the work of looking out for church members falls exclusively on church staff, with the inevitable consequence that people fall through the gaps, often at the times they most need input. We should never underestimate the needs in an average church for encouraging and supportive input, however outwardly confident people seem. Proverbs 14:10 tells us that 'Each heart knows its own bitterness' – some hearts more than others of course, but it certainly implies a great deal of work is to be done to minister to people and to encourage them to focus not on their disappointments but on Christ.

But how do we make these times more than just a catch-up about our weekend activities, or sport or our health problems? How do we make our conversations count for eternity? They need to be centred on things that count for eternity - on the Lord Jesus, on the gospel and its application to our life. The challenge is to move conversation on to a deeper level in a natural way that encourages honesty. The key to this is to be proactive and to be prepared to *ask focused questions* that will centre the conversation on spiritual issues.

Whether we are meeting with an old friend or someone we don't know well, we will want to have a genuine interest in where they are coming from and what they are going through. As we get to know someone well, we become more comfortable about sharing the key issues of the moment with one another without prompting. If the relationship is good we will be able to determine quite quickly where the needs are as they come up in conversation. Perhaps a new job might mean our friend is looking for advice on workplace evangelism, a health problem might require reminders to be patient, prayerful and heaven focused, while a new relationship might call for a brief discussion on that issue.

We need to have eternity as our perspective, so that when we ask questions, we will not merely think, 'Will they like being asked this or not?' but rather, 'Will they thank me for asking this question in ten thousand years from now?' But, we will need to ask such questions with great sensitivity. The better we know people the bolder we can be in our questioning, but we should always beware of straying into territory where we are not welcome. We can ask, 'Do you mind me asking about X or Y?' which will give them freedom to say they would rather not talk about that subject. When we sense we are treading where our friend does not want us to go, we should change the subject, but note the issue to see if it is something that can be discussed next time. There may be a bigger issue, which can be talked about when the relationship is stronger.

What, though, of their walk with Jesus? This will be the key area to talk about. As they talk through their use of time, is Jesus getting a respectable amount of it for times of devotion, growth and service? In a time of uncertainty, are they trusting Jesus whatever the outcome, and committing it to him in prayer? In a time of success and achievement, is Jesus getting the glory, or is their pride the pre-eminent factor?

One way of moving the conversation into the area of our relationship with God is to ask about what they have been learning from the teaching they have been receiving: 'Is there anything that has really struck you from the sermon series on Joshua/from your Bible studies in Romans/from your quiet times recently?' Or, 'Are you finding that what you are learning in Romans is reshaping your priorities and perspective in any way?' We should also invite them to ask the same questions of us. In this way we are making the most of our conversation – focusing on the gospel and how it is changing us, rather than merely on the superficial.

Three golden questions

I have three key questions up my sleeve when meeting up with someone from my Bible study group or dormitory at 'camp'. Time and time again I've found that one of the three gets to the heart of the issue and reveals enough about that person's Christian understanding enabling one to see how I can best help them and lead them forward. (The first two are taken from the Christianity Explored course.)

Question 1: '*If God were here, and you could ask him any question (and you knew that he would give you a straight answer) what would you ask?*' This is particularly useful in opening up a discussion with someone who isn't a Christian.

Question 2: '*Suppose later on today you're crossing the road, and you get hit by the number 17 bus, and you die (sorry about that, but just imagine) and you meet God, and he asks you, "Why should I let you into my heaven?" What would you say?*' This is really good at revealing whether someone is trusting in Jesus, and in salvation by grace alone, or whether he or she has begun to rely on their own good works to take them to heaven.

Question 3: '*Supposing you were a junior demon, and the devil assigned you the task of*

> *tempting [insert their name], and messing up his/her Christian life. What would you go for?'* A more searching and intimate question that needs to be used with care. But it is an opportunity for someone to seek your help with a particular struggle that they're going through.

Often, however, we will need to do the potentially harder work of helping someone have a proper biblical understanding in times of specific problems and challenges, or a battle with sin, as well as when things are going well for them. The temptation in tough times is to take our eyes off Jesus, focus on the problem, and lose confidence in our Saviour. Our job is to help one another to 'fix [our] eyes on Jesus' (Heb.12:2), the one who endured the greatest hardship for us, and to remember that we are on our way to where he is now – heaven.

The rest of this chapter will deal with how to help people in different circumstances, facing different struggles or challenges. Any input we give needs to be done with great care, being mindful of all the issues and factors affecting a person. We must be gracious with people, not quick to condemn, and we should not be unrealistic in our expectations. If a friend has just been through a hard time, inevitably their guard may have dropped in some areas. If they are a new Christian, we should not expect them to take a lead role in service. If they are finding it hard to get to a good church because of distance, we should not berate them for it, but be willing to get involved personally in providing alternatives, like sending a weekly tape or recommending an Internet site with good sermons, or even trying to organize a lift for them. We must have a genuine concern for people that leads to loving words and loving actions which seek to build them up in their walk with the Lord Jesus.

Once we have asked questions, one of the most important things we must do with someone in our 'care' is to be genuinely interested in what they have to say. We need to *listen* carefully and compassionately to his or her struggles, fears and hopes. Our temptation is to say far too much – to want to correct someone with thousands of well-thought-through words. But often only one thing is appropriate and sufficient. We need to wait, reflect and then gently and considerately offer one or two helpful things to our friend, encouraging them to spend good time digesting them. Maybe if they want advice over a situation, ask, 'What would you say to someone else facing your situation?' to help them start preaching the truth to themselves.

2. Encouragement

Some will need *encouraging or comforting* because of difficult circumstances such as a bereavement (which may come in a number of forms of change and/or loss), or being worn out after doing too much at home, work or church. In the case of bereavement it may be worth speaking to an older Christian or church staff member, suggest some helpful Scriptures, or find a book to help them through the issues. The Psalms – number 89 onwards in particular – contain much material to help people through hard times. They allow us to express our mixed emotions to God, through the psalmist's cries, and can help us to *feel* the truths that God cares for us and is in control. It's striking how in 2 Thessalonians 2:16 we are told that Jesus himself and God gave us 'eternal encouragement'. We must not be afraid of taking people back to the biblical teaching about heaven, a place with no more death, mourning, crying or pain (Rev. 21:4), when dealing with dire circumstances.

But we must be careful of simply offering platitudes like 'God loves you, so all will be OK'. We need to express that love though our actions. A prolonged period of discouragement may take time to overcome. We need to be mindful that depressive illness of some kind may have set in, and seek advice on how to handle this (see chapter 7). Our responsibility, facing any issue in conversation with someone, is to use biblical knowledge to shape what we say. We are not counsellors, and should not pretend to claim expertise in areas that are normally the domain of professionals.

One conversation can turn your mind around

She said one thing, which I will never forget, 'Remember what happened to Jonah!' I had just had my engagement called off and I was desperate. It had all felt so 'right' and I couldn't understand why this break-up was happening. My big concern was, 'What if he (my ex-fiance) was running away from God's will?' My friend sat there and listened to my ranting and comforted me and then just said, 'But remember what happened to Jonah when he tried to run away from God's will? If it's right, then God will bring him back round.' Really simply and clearly (and rather amusingly), my friend had pointed me back to God's word and it turned out to be one of the major milestones on my road to acceptance and forgiveness, as I was challenged to trust in God's sovereignty over the situation.

3. Rebuke

We may have occasion to *rebuke* someone whom we meet with. This has to be done with great care, and we should follow Paul's example once again, and do so 'in love' as Ephesians 4:15 suggests. It is an accepted reality that we are all fallen and that we cannot rule out the prospect of stubborn rebellion or coming under the influence of a false doctrine. Often we may not realize it, and sometimes circumstances may mean it has been difficult to avoid – for instance, a set of new friends at a new university can exert heavy pressure on a young Christian to do a variety of things they may not have wanted to do.

In most cases, a gentle encouraging word, backed up with tactfully given biblical evidence will show the error of one's ways, and people will make suitable changes. Handled well, the word 'rebuke' need never be mentioned or associated with such a time at all. It might be worth looking up in a concordance all the verses featuring the word '*gentle*' before we embark on this work! Verses such as 1 Corinthians 4:21, Ephesians 4:2, 1 Timothy 3:3 and many of the Proverbs can really help us.

It is also useful to establish how they regard their situation before we step in with our comments. Do they recognize the situation as wrong in God's view? There is often ambivalence, when in our heart we suspect something is not right but try to rationalize and justify it to ourselves. If the opposite is true and they are overwhelmed by how they could have done/thought such a thing, a rebuke may not be necessary – rather, helping them to see the extent of God's grace may be more appropriate. We can point them to the failings of those characters in the Bible who God blessed and used most such as King David, a known adulterer, and the apostle Peter, who denied friendship with Jesus three times.

If we have to rebuke we should be careful of our own place, ensuring we are not guilty of the same sin (Mt. 7:3–5), and that we don't find ourselves being dragged into the same sin (Gal. 6:1). Only in certain cases and with consultation with church leaders should we seek to be more demanding and direct with someone who continues in a sin and who we suspect has hardened their hearts to God's word (see Matthew 18:15–20 for a model on how to do this).

4. Correction

On other occasions, *correction* is called for where you encounter false doctrine or a mistaken view of salvation. Proverbs 15:32 says, 'Whoever heeds correction gains understanding.' The

Christian needs to be on the look out for false doctrines, as throughout history these have crept in with amazing regularity, and sadly can spread quickly (2 Tim. 2:17; Tit. 1:11; 2 Pet. 2:1). It is important that we are constantly seeking to improve our own knowledge of Scripture so that we can spot these errors. The person we meet for one-to-one could attend a university group where false teaching is present, or may, through a group of friends, have come under the influence of some form of new teaching which is not Christ-centred or biblical.

Helping as forgiven sinners

A friend and I found it much easier to honestly correct and rebuke one another once we came to terms with the doctrine of total depravity – that is, the truth that every area of our lives is contaminated by sin. I didn't have any trouble believing it about myself! I just had trouble believing it about my friend – he seemed so nice! It turned out that he felt the same way about me. But once we came to terms with what the Bible said about each other, we started being much more honest. We realized that we couldn't shock each other with the reality of our sin, because it was no more than the Bible already told us. So we could stop hiding behind the pharisaic veneer of a sorted Christian life and start really helping one another as forgiven sinners.

The basis for *any* rebuke or correction must be the Bible. This is, after all, what 2 Timothy 3:16 says it is useful for! We must remember, though, that the Bible is God's word – so any time we use the Bible to rebuke or correct we are doing so in God's name, and we must not bring dishonour to that name by doing it carelessly or improperly. If we think someone has got some doctrine wrong, we should always check our own position first – are we the one in error perhaps? It may be a secondary issue, which simply requires our one-to-one partner being taught both sides of the argument so they can make their own mind up. Where the error is more significant – a salvation issue perhaps – and the person seems stuck in their ways, we should refer the matter to a church leader, and pray for them. Prevention is better than cure: if we can teach people to be discerning, we may be able to immunize them against false doctrine before it turns up.

5. Challenge

Lastly, we may be called to *challenge* someone – to consider, as it says in Hebrews 10:24, how we can 'spur one another on towards love and good deeds'. The person we meet with may have things going pretty smoothly and under control in their lives. This means there is probably capacity for them to do a little bit more – to try something new, like showing their love for fellow church members by participating in some service or starting to lead a small group, or even meeting someone else for one-to-one. The fact is that they may never have thought that they were ready to start something new themselves. Often, we just need some encouragement from an older Christian to have a go at some new area of service.

We need to do as Hebrews 10 says and carefully consider what might be right for the person concerned. Is now a good time for them to start something new? Is this really the right thing for them? Suggest the right thing, and provide encouragement along the way, and your challenge to get started could lead your one-to-one partner into a lifetime of fulfilled, God-honouring Christian service.

6. Bible passages for specific issues

Sometimes it will be entirely appropriate to open the Bible and look at a specific passage together. The following is a list of some of the issues or struggles that we may all face at different times of our lives and some parts of Scripture which address these issues either directly or indirectly. When opening one of these passages with someone, often just reading it together with time to mull is sufficient. Questions like, 'What do you find helpful/challenging in here?' or, 'What would our lives look like if we really believed this?' are always useful to have up your sleeve.

- **Depression/heartbreak**
  Lots of the Psalms! e.g. Psalm 34:18; 42; 147:3
  Romans 8:18–39
- **Fear**
  Psalm 23
  Romans 8:31–39
  Hebrews 13:5–6
- **Forgiveness and forgiving others**
  Psalm 51
  Matthew 6:9-15; 18:21–23
  Luke 15:11–24
  Colossians 3:12–14
  1 John 1:8–9
- **Grief/Bereavement**
  2 Corinthians 1:3–4
  1 Thessalonians 4:13–18
  Revelation 21:4
- **Guidance**
  Psalm 25; 32:8–11
  Proverbs 3:5–6; 16:9
  James 1:5–8

- **Quiet Time**
  Psalm 1
  Psalm 119:1–116
- **Worry**
  Matthew 6:25–34
  Philippians 4:6-7, 12–13
  1 Peter 5:6–7

Study guide

- Thinking about Christians you know in a particular age group or setting – the Christian Union, youth group, etc. – what issues do you think they most need help with? What Bible passages would you take them to, to address each issue you have come up with?
- Think through what sort of input you might want from an older or friendly Christian in a time of a) bereavement, b) start of a new relationship, c) unemployment or exam disappointment, d) relationship breakdown.
- Who in your church/CU/work fellowship could most do with some encouragement from the Scriptures? Who is best placed to encourage them in this way? Why not you?
- If someone were reading the Bible with you, what challenge, rebuke or encouragement would you most like or need to get at the moment? How would you go about giving it to yourself?

Something to do: Ask someone in your church or fellowship who has recently been through hard times what input they would most have wanted in the midst of their struggles. What Bible texts would have been an encouragement?

7

Other Considerations

1. Accountability

One-to-one work is, by nature, hidden from the public eye, and it is thus very important to ensure that you are transparent and accountable in the light of all the dangers mentioned in chapter 2. You need to check that you are not teaching heresy or being legalistic. Others need to ask you how your responsibility of prayer is going and whether you are being open and honest with your one-to-one partner. You need to check whether you are giving appropriate advice in response to sensitive situations. Someone else also needs to check whether you are being 'drained' by a demanding or dependent person.

This sort of accountability can be achieved in a number of ways. The most common is to have a prayer partner or be part of a prayer triplet. These usually (though not necessarily) emerge out of existing strong friendships, where all members agree to make a commitment to meet fairly regularly to share struggles, burdens, and encouragements so they can then pray through these things together. As trust develops, members should be able to ask each other probing questions about their relationship with God, relationships with others, any particular issues they are known to struggle with and also how their ministry is going. This, of course, raises the issue of confidentiality between you and your one-to-one partner, which needs to be discussed (see section 2 below), but this sort of committed support can be a vital encouragement and check alongside your one-to-one ministry.

It is also important, however, that someone in leadership of your church, small group, Christian Union or youth group, knows that you are meeting up with another person from the fellowship. They can then ask you the right questions (do encourage them to) and be available to speak with you if any major issues arise.

2. Pastoral issues

Confidentiality

It is important that you are an utterly trust- worthy confidante to your one-to-one partner.

Generally it is a good thing to discuss the issue of confidentiality with one another during your first meeting together. It is usually not necessary or advisable to promise one another confidentiality for everything that is said between you. We should be aware that we must never promise confidentiality to anyone under the age of eighteen years – we are obliged under law to report any incidents of abuse that are claimed by minors (under-eighteens). We are also obliged under law to report any criminal acts that are disclosed to us by people of any age. In addition to knowing these things ourselves, we need to make our one-to-one partners aware of the fact that we are under these legal obligations. We should, however, be loyal and discreet about what has been shared with us and avoid gossip at all costs.

As you grow in trust with one another, it is very possible that major, long-standing issues may arise. These may include psychological, physical and/or sexual abuse from childhood, eating disorders, self-harm, depression and sexuality issues, to mention but a few. Our first reaction can often be one of shock and fear and a sense of total helplessness. Although these are totally normal responses, it is important to try and keep these reactions internal as they might make the sharer feel intimidated and unable to open up any further. If possible, stay very calm and appear unshockable! A loving, non-judgemental, listening ear is worth everything in such circumstances. But be wary of encouraging them to open up further over issues such as past abuse. Before doing so you may need to clarify with them that you would like to talk to someone with more experience of these things at church for your own support in best helping them. It is unwise and can be unhelpful to promise confidentiality when dealing with really major psychological problems, because they may end up becoming very dependent on you and need more emotional support than you can provide. You will need others to advise, protect and pray for you in these situations.

God's sovereignty, our responsibility

We must always remember the truth of God's loving sovereignty and ultimate responsibility to take care of his children. Knowing this will give us more confidence to keep persevering with someone who is sharing some distressing personal struggles, without that sense of panic at our total inexperience or sense of helplessness. We can sit with them as they talk and cry and wrestle with their emotions, and all the while be silently praying (and at appropriate times praying with them) for God's wisdom and strength to help us be a good friend to them, and for him to be working his purposes out in their life. It is God's commitment 'in all things [to work] for the good of those who love him, who have been called according to his purpose' (Rom. 8:28), and to keep his sheep from being snatched from Jesus' hands (Jn. 10:29). We must look to him to keep his people, to not let them be tested beyond what they can bear (1 Cor. 10:13), and to give them the strength to persevere.

For our part, we will need God's help as we seek the necessary love and patience to keep listening to the same expressions of confusion or despair, often over a period of many months (or even years), as the person slowly comes to terms with their struggle – whether heartache, bereavement or serious illness. Part of genuine love for our Christian brothers and sisters is the act of gently coming alongside them in their hard times and '[mourning] with those who mourn' (Rom. 12:15).

True compassion is when someone willingly puts themselves in another's shoes and experiences their pain and anguish with them; someone who chooses to join with another in their hour of need and share some of the burden with them. This can be very costly. It means giving precious time to someone in need when this time will rarely benefit you in any earthly terms. It can be emotionally draining 'being there' for someone who needs ongoing support and attention, but it can be extremely helpful and healing for the person being supported. Dr

Ros Furlong, a consultant psychiatrist, has commented that the expressing of emotion can often reduce the depressing (generally and clinically) build-up of unexpressed pain and/or anger. Therefore just allowing this is in itself helpful, even when we cannot find answers or effective comforting words.

It is also important to check to what extent the rest of the family of an individual are involved in helping them cope with their struggles. Wherever possible we should seek to support and strengthen the role of the immediate family – whether Christian or non-Christian – in caring for an individual, so that we are not seen as threatening or undermining those key relationships in any way. We should also seek to involve others in the church family in the care of individuals, where appropriate. For example, if we know someone else in the congregation has gone through a very similar traumatic experience to the person we are meeting with, then maybe we can ask both parties if they would be willing to meet with one another to talk things through.

Dealing with tears

People cry for all sorts of reasons – release of emotional tension, conviction of sin, desire to manipulate, grief. If someone bursts into tears on me I have to tell myself not to panic or over-react (e.g. thinking that it's my fault that I've upset them), but to hand them a tissue, put an arm around their shoulders where appropriate, and give them time to gather themselves together before giving them time to talk.

Tears of grief/mourning are a little different. When I sat with someone who was weeping with griefthat had because of some devastating thing happened to her, I found that all I could do was hold her hand and cry with her. Words didn't seem appropriate because the situation was so awful and tragic, and I guess that just being there was all I could do for that half an hour. I think that this is what the Bible means about weeping and mourning with those who weep and mourn.

When and how to get professional (counselling) help

From Disciplemaker's Handbook by Alice Fryling, IVP 1989

The question is often asked, 'How do I know when someone needs professional help?' The following symptoms may indicate that you are dealing with problems too difficult to handle alone:

- the problem persists for many months, with no resolution in sight;
- they feel as if they 'have all the answers' but don't know how to apply them to their situation;
- they feel very depressed for several weeks at a time for no apparent reason;
- thoughts of suicide or other abnormal behaviour intrude frequently into their thinking;
- they have developed a persistent problem with sleep – this is a good practical guide and can also be a cause as well as an effect. [This last point added by Dr Ros Furlong.]

If professional counselling is necessary, the following suggestions may help in finding a suitable counsellor.

- The relationship between the counsellor and client is very unique and very intimate – they need to look for someone they feel comfortable with. If the first counsellor doesn't work out, look for another. But remember it sometimes takes a while to establish trust, especially contrasting the new relationship with the trust already built up with you.
- Ask a friend, a minister, a doctor or someone else you respect for a recommendation for a good counsellor.

- Get them to try to speak with the counsellor by phone before the first appointment. Even a phone conversation will give an idea of whether or not they will be able to relate to the counsellor. They should ask about his or her professional certification, and ask what approach the counsellor uses. Ask about the person's professional background (this should tell you how much experience the person has had in counselling). Ask too how the counsellor's spiritual values influence his or her counselling.
- It is best if the counsellor is a believer, but don't assume that a non-Christian counsellor cannot be helpful. Likewise don't assume that just because someone is a Christian he or she will be a good counsellor.
- Once they begin to see the counsellor, get them to ask for an assessment of their situation and the counsellor's tentative goals for their counselling experience. The counsellor won't be able to hand them 'all the answers' but should have insights and be concerned that they achieve appropriate goals.
- When someone goes for counselling, they should be as open, as honest and as specific as they can be about their own needs and feelings. Their participation in their counselling experience is even more important than the counsellor's in terms of the success of the therapy.

It is worth stressing, however, that even if someone is getting psychological/medical help from a doctor or counsellor, that doesn't mean they won't at the same time benefit from spiritual and biblical help from you. Mental health problems aside, it is only by 'learning Christ' that we will be 'made new in the attitude of [our] minds' (Eph. 4:23) and for all their expertise, we would be unwise to trust many counsellors to maintain that gospel focus. Even in hard situations, people will still need reminding of what they know, and correcting, albeit gently. And they may need comfort and encouragement as they submit to God's care, discipline, truth and wisdom in a fallen world.

3. Moving on

This should be an exciting time as we see our one-to-one partner move on to live the Christian life more confidently and to serve the church more effectively as they are more rooted and established in Christ. There should be a shift in the nature of the friendship that has been anticipated right at the outset. However, it can also be a very tricky issue indeed. People can end up feeling if the change in the terms of the relationship isn't anticipated or handled wisely. It is not always possible to avoid misunderstandings or differing expectations as you stop meeting to look at the Bible together regularly. People can easily become hurt if the nature of the friendship, and the fact that the regular meeting will not go on for ever, aren't explained up front. This is especially (though not exclusively) the case with younger people – school children or students. They can easily assume they have a new friend and 'guardian' for life and if their mentor then moves on after a year or two with no explanation, the young Christian can feel bewildered and even rejected.

Although it is often the case that long-term friendships do develop out of a one-to-one arrangement, especially between peers, this does not always happen. In such instances there will need to be a 'cooling off' period in the relationship where you no longer meet every week or fortnight but less frequently and in a more informal way (see previous chapter on 'meeting occasionally') where you still have some sense of pastoral responsibility for them. This moving on may occur naturally when you have finished looking at a book of the Bible or a series of studies, or it may be when the agreed time span is 'up'. Moving on from here is so much easier if you have anticipated it at the start of the relationship (see chapter 4) and explained that your desire for them is to move on from your meetings, equipped to serve others in the church.

We will want to ensure that our ex-one-to-one partner has a number of other Christian friendships that will keep them persevering in their faith. Are they a member of a home group or other small group? Are they going to start meeting with another friend to pray together and keep each other accountable? Are they involved in some sort of work of service at church, such as welcoming, catering or leading a one-to-one or small group Bible study? These are the sorts of questions to work through with them as you stop meeting regularly. However, we must continue to be genuinely concerned for our ex-one-to-one partners – phone calls, cards, emails, catching up at church and so on, should be part of ongoing loving care for our Christian brother or sister, as we seek to encourage them to live for God. Hopefully this ongoing care will be very much mutual.

Moving on is not just an issue for the person we've been meeting with, however. We might find that we struggle to truly 'let them go'. There is always a temptation to enjoy being looked up to and needed and so to encourage ongoing dependence on us for support and guidance. Our longing should be, however, that they grow more and more dependent on God and his word in all matters and that they form a number of lasting Christian friendships to encourage them to keep going. We should long to see them reach their full potential in serving God and not feel threatened if they go on to leadership positions to which we have to submit or teaching ministries from which we can really learn! Ananias and Barnabas saw the man they were involved in discipling become the great apostle to the Gentiles and author of much of the New Testament. What would have happened if they had wanted Paul to stay under their influence and not surpass them in leadership?

There are times when we are lazy or lacking in genuine concern for individuals and need to be challenged to continue to care for a brother or sister in the Lord out of sincere love for them – to check they are going well in their Christian life and still trusting in Jesus. There are other times when our worry for individuals or sense of guilt in not seeing them is borne more out of pride and a lack of trust in God to work in his people, than out of sincere love. This is when we need to remember Philippians 1:6 where Paul is 'confident of this, that he who began a good work in you will carry it on to completion until the day of Christ Jesus'. We need to be able to let go of our sense of prime responsibility for individuals as we see them become rooted and established in Christ. This is what we were aiming for in our one-to-one ministry after all!

Study guide

- If someone asked whether they could be accountable to you, in their work of discipling a younger Christian, what things would you be looking out for?
- What structures for accountability are there in your church, Christian Union or work fellowship? Do you need to suggest some to the leadership?
- Apart from having someone specific overseeing us, how else can we ensure transparency when we are meeting one-to-one?
- In this chapter it was suggested that 'True compassion is when someone willingly puts themselves in another's shoes and experiences their pain and anguish with them.' What will this mean in practice?

Something to do: Ask your church or fellowship leader if an accountability group could be set up to support those doing one-to-one. If one already exists, ask them what things they most look out for.

8

Resources

1. Study resources

The Good Book Company study guides are an excellent place to start. For example:

- *The Complete Christian* (Colossians)
- *The Path to Godliness* (Titus)
- *Full of Promise* (Old Testament overview)
- *The Blueprint* (Christian doctrine)
- *Bold I Approach* (Studies on prayer)

They have also recently produced a book called *One2One – 24 Studies for Bible Reading Partnerships* by Andrew Cornes, which contains studies in John 13 – 16, Philippians and Psalms.

C. Marshall's, *Growth Groups: A Training Course in How to Lead Small Groups* (London: St Matthias Press, 1995) is a resource primarily for group Bible studies, but has some very helpful material on how to prepare and lead studies, and contains sample study preparation material on Colossians.

To order:

- online at www.thegoodbookcompany.co.uk
- email at admin@thegoodbook.co.uk
- telephone on: +44 (0)20 8942 0880
- fax to: +44 (0)20 8942 0990.

Courses for new Christians

Just for Starters – seven basic Bible studies or *Firm Foundations*, which is an expanded version of *Just for Starters*. Topics covered: the cross, grace, life by the Spirit, Bible study, prayer, God's family, evangelism. This material is available from The Good Book Company (see above).

Gospel Truths to Live By – a course of eight Bible studies. Topics covered: grace, the cross, life by the Spirit, the cost of discipleship, sex, evangelism, money, perseverance. This material is produced by St Andrew the Great Church, Cambridge email: staff@stag.org.

Three sample studies for (new) Christians – from Colossians

Study 1: Introduction and overview

1. *Who is the letter from? What is the significance of the title Paul gives himself?* (OBSERVATION)

- The apostle Paul and Timothy.
- An 'apostle' was someone personally commissioned by Jesus to speak for him (cf. 1:25).

2. *What do we know about Paul from the letter?* (OBSERVATION)

- He is in chains (4:3, 18), in prison (4:10).
- He has never met them personally (1:9; 2:1).
- He labours in preaching the gospel to Gentiles (1:28, 29).
- He suffers a lot for his ministry (1:24).

3. *Who is the letter to and what do we learn about them from the letter?* (OBSERVATION)

- The Colossian church – but also to be read by the Laodicean church (4:16).
- They heard the gospel through Epaphras, who was from Colossae (1:7; 4:12).
- They are going strong in their faith (1:3-5; 2:5).
- But there are some false teachers around (2:8, 16, 18).

4. *What do you think is Paul's purpose in writing? Look out for any recurring themes or ideas.* (INTERPRETATION)

- He encourages them to keep going in Christ.
- He warns them about false teachers leading them away from Jesus.

- He teaches them why Jesus is solely sufficient to save them.
- He wants them to live out their faith in Christ effectively.

5. *Summarize the dangers/threats that Paul seems to be concerned about.* (INTERPRETATION)

- There were people saying that you need something more than just faith in Christ (e.g. you must keep the law/follow rules/have special experiences) to experience the 'fullness' of a relationship with God.

6. *In some ways, 2:6–7 sums up the central theme of the letter. What do you think is the significance of the two words 'just as' (NIV)?* (INTERPRETATION)

- Paul is telling the Colossians to stick with the message that they first believed, to go on in the Christian life in just the same way as they started, to hold on to Jesus and not to deviate to anything new.

7. *How would you sum up Paul's aim in writing to the Colossians?* (APPLICATION TO THEM)

- You have fullness in Christ – don't look anywhere else!

8. *What do you think are going to be the big applications of this letter to us?* (APPLICATION TO US)

- We need to realize that we have fullness in Christ – and not look anywhere else!

Study 2: Colossians 1:1–8

1. *Why does Paul start his letter in this way – i.e. stress his apostleship?*

- So they accept what he is about to say is from God and utterly trustworthy – he will clear up the confusion surrounding the different teaching going on in Colossae.

2. *What two things is Paul thankful for in the lives of the Colossians?* (OBSERVATION)

- Faith (i.e. trust) in Jesus and love for other Christians ('saints') (1:4).
- Note that this love is not just for particular favourites, but also for 'all'.

3. *Where does Paul say these qualities come from?* (OBSERVATION)

- Their faith and love spring from the hope that is laid up for them in heaven, v5. This promise of inheritance (v12) in heaven comes through the message that they heard, i.e. the gospel, v5. So the gospel tells them of the promise of final salvation and this leads them to put their faith in Jesus and to love other followers of Jesus.

4. *Why do you think Paul puts the emphasis on the hope? (Think of context/theme)* (INTERPRETATION)

- Because he wants them to see that the gospel is fundamentally about faith in a future hope, so they must keep on going (cf. 1:23).

5. *Why do you think we don't emphasize hope as we should today?* (APPLICATION TO US)

- We don't like waiting for things, we want it all now – we are impatient.

6. *How would Paul's words have reassured the Colossians in the face of false teachers who were questioning the validity of their religious experience?* (INTERPRETATION)

- Paul, the apostle, is thanking God for them. Evidently Paul can see that their faith is the real McCoy.
- Faith in Christ Jesus, love for other Christians and the hope of heaven are the marks of genuine Christian experience. There is no need for anything extra, whatever the false teachers might have said.

7. In what different ways does Paul describe the message that Epaphras brought to the Colossians? What do they mean? (OBSERVATION AND INTERPRETATION)

- 'word of truth' – it's true!
- 'gospel' – the word means good news.
- 'God's grace in all its truth' – this message is about God's grace, i.e. his undeserved favour shown to sinners.

8. Paul says that the Colossians 'heard' (1:5) and 'understood (1:6) and 'learned' (1:7) a message. That doesn't seem very impressive in comparison with the amazing spiritual experiences the false teachers were claiming. But what is the result of this hearing? (INTERPRETATION)

- This message has produced faith, love and hope in the Colossians.
- And it's bearing fruit all over the world (1:6).
- It may not look very spectacular, but hearing and understanding the word of God is life changing!

9. To summarize, how does Paul reassure the Colossians that their Christian experience is the real thing? (APPLICATION TO THEM)

- Whatever the false teachers might say, there is no more-genuine Christian experience than that which comes from hearing and understanding God's word and putting it into practice in your life.

- The gospel that they first heard and responded to is the same gospel that is bearing fruit all over the world.

10. *According to the passage, what signs should we look for in our own lives to see whether our Christian experience is genuine?* (APPLICATION TO US)

- We should check that our Christian experience is rooted in an understanding of God's word of truth.
- We should check that this message is bearing fruit in our lives – especially the fruit of a confident hope of heaven, a love for Christian brothers and sisters and a deep trust in Jesus.

11. *How might that reassure us when other people speak of dramatic spiritual experiences that make us feel inferior?* (APPLICATION TO US)

- If anyone comes along promising a deeper experience of God, or some special secret of spiritual progress, we should treat it with profound scepticism. We've already got all we need in Jesus.

Study 3: Colossians 1:9–14

1. *What is the connection between this passage and what we looked at last time? Why is Paul motivated to pray for people whom he's never met?* (OBSERVATION AND INTERPRETATION)

- Verse 9 begins with the words 'for this reason', meaning we should look back at verses 3–8.
- We learnt last time that the Colossians are genuine Christians with a genuine Christian experience. That is why Paul has not stopped praying for them.
- It's striking that we often pray only when we know someone is in trouble. Paul seems rather to pray for the Colossians because they are doing so well!

2. *At first sight it looks like quite a complicated prayer, but if we look closely, there's only one thing that Paul actually asks for. What is it?* (OBSERVATION)

- Paul asks God to fill the Colossians with a knowledge of God's will (1:9). Everything else flows from that.

3. *'Knowing God's will' is a much misunderstood phrase. How does it fit in with the theme of the letter?* (INTERPRETATION)

- We often think of God's will in terms of a particular blueprint for our life – whether we should be a sailor or a schoolteacher; whether we should marry Pauline or Patricia, Patrick or Peter.
- In the bigger context of Colossians, however, 'God's will' probably refers to the gospel – God's plan of salvation – because this is what Paul goes on to teach them more about in 1:13–23, and also because he tells them the way to grow in Christ is to continue in him 'as [they] were taught' (2:6–7), which is by the gospel message (1:5).
- So it is knowing and understanding the gospel better which will lead the Colossians to live a life worthy of the Lord.

4. *What different things does knowing the gospel better lead to?* (OBSERVATION)

- 'bearing fruit in every good work' (1:10) Note this is connected to 1:6
- 'growing in the knowledge of God' (1:10)
- 'being strengthened with all power' (1:11)
- 'joyfully giving thanks to the Father' (1:12)

5. *'Power' and 'strength' (1:11) may well have been buzzwords among the impressive false teachers in Colossae. What is surprising though about how true power and strength are shown?* (INTERPRETATION)

- Power and strength are needed for 'endurance and patience' (1:11). It might have looked unspectacular by comparison with whatever the false teachers were promising, but Paul is clear that the mere fact of Christians keeping going in their faith is a work of God's mighty strength.

6. *What reasons does Paul give in verses 12–13 for joyfully giving thanks? Pay attention to which things are in the past and which are in the present tense!* (OBSERVATION AND INTERPRETATION)

- We have been qualified (1:12) – there will be no exam for entry into heaven. Jesus has done the work for us already (past tense). But what we have been qualified for is something in the future – to share in the inheritance of the saints (future hope).
- We have been rescued (1:13) (past tense). The transfer from the dominion of darkness into the kingdom of the Son he loves is something that is already complete for anyone who is a Christian.
- We have redemption and the forgiveness of sins (1:14) (present tense). Our ongoing experience as Christians is that of being set free by Jesus and having daily access to the forgiveness he offers.

7. *To summarize, what is the one thing that Paul wants for the Colossians that underpins everything else?* (APPLICATION TO THEM)

- Paul longs for the Colossians more and more to grasp God's will for them in the gospel. All else flows from that.

8. What is the fundamental thing that Paul would want for us? (APPLICATION TO US)

- He would want us to know God's will for us in the gospel, so that we might live a life worthy of him, pleasing him in every way – bearing fruit in every good work, growing in the knowledge of God, being strengthened with all power to keep going, joyfully giving thanks to the Father for all he has done for us in Jesus.

9. What is the fundamental thing we should pray for Christian friends? (APPLICATION TO US)

- This would be a great prayer for us to pray for one another. And not just for those who are struggling, but for Christians who are living out the genuine Christian life.

Two sample studies for non-Christians – from Mark's Gospel[6]

Mark 2:1–12

Read the passage aloud and then work through the study below. The answers are printed here for your reference. The 'Additional notes for leaders' section may also help you.

Focus In

1. *The passage opens by telling us that so many people had gathered to hear Jesus that there was no room left. Why had so many people come to hear Jesus? (Look at Mark 1:27–28, 32–34, 45 for clues.)*

- Jesus' teaching and healing has amazed people and news about him was spreading.

2. *Why did these people bring their friend to Jesus?*

- To have him healed of his paralysis.

3. *In view of the situation, what is surprising about what Jesus says in Mark 2:5?*

- Jesus says, 'Son, your sins are forgiven.' The man was lowered through the roof in order that he might be healed, not have his sins forgiven.

4. *Why were the teachers of the law so annoyed about Jesus' remark? (See Mark 2:6–7.)*

- Jesus is claiming to do that which only God can do, something the teachers of the law see clearly (Mk. 2:7). So they conclude that he is blaspheming.

5. *Were they right?*

- Yes and no. Yes, only God can forgive sin. No, Jesus isn't blaspheming because he is God.

6. How do we know that Jesus has authority to forgive sin? (See Mark 2:8–12.)

- He healed the man.

7. What does this incident imply about who Jesus is? (See Mark 2:7.)

- He is God. ('Who can forgive sins but God alone?')

8. Why do you think Jesus said, 'Son, your sins are forgiven' before healing the man?

- The man's greatest need is to have his sins forgiven, not to be healed. Note: This is because – as we shall see in the next study – sin determines our eternal destination.

Additional Notes for Leaders

- **Blasphemy (Mk. 2:7)**

Only God can forgive sin because God is the one against whom we rebel. So when Jesus claims to forgive sin, he is putting himself in God's place. The religious authorities see this as blasphemy – a slander against God. Either Jesus is a blasphemer or, if Jesus is God, then the teachers of the law are the ones guilty of blasphemy!

- **Son of Man (Mk. 2:10)**

This is Jesus' way of referring to himself. It recalls Daniel 7:9-14 in which the 'son of man' was the name of the one who approached the Ancient of Days (i.e. God), and was given authority to rule over everyone forever, starting from the final judgement. In this world, however, far from ruling, he must suffer and die. Thus, 'Son of Man' is a title that embodies all that Jesus wants to teach the disciples about himself.

Mark 4:35–41

1. *Why are the disciples afraid in Mark 4:37–38?*

- They think they are going to die. Remember, some of the disciples are experienced fishermen; they're not easily frightened.

2. *What is so remarkable about the way in which Jesus calms the storm? (See Mark 4:39.)*

- He did it with a few simple words. The fact that Jesus instantly calmed not just the furious wind, but the huge waves as well – even though waves normally persist for hours or even days after the wind dies down shows that a miracle has taken place.

3. *What is surprising about Jesus' response to the disciples? (See Mark 4:40.)*

- He rebukes them for being frightened of losing their lives. He tells them they should have faith.

4. Why don't the disciples have faith, i.e. why don't they trust Jesus? (See Mark 4:41.)

- They don't know who he is.

5. What should the disciples have understood from this incident bearing in mind they were Jews who would have been steeped in the Old Testament? (One of the leaders should read aloud these verses as examples of what the disciples would have known – Psalm 65:5–7: 89:9; 107:23–30.)

- The Old Testament is clear that only God has power and authority over the wind and waves. They should have seen that Jesus is God.

6. How would you answer the disciples' question in Mark 4:41: 'Who is this? Even the wind and the waves obey him!'

- This question is designed to reveal whether the participants have grasped who Jesus is. Rather than pressing them for an answer, it may be more appropriate for participants to reflect on this in their own time.

Additional Notes for Leaders

- **'Do you still have no faith?' (Mk. 4:40)**

Despite all the evidence they've witnessed, the disciples still don't have faith in Jesus. (Note: to 'have faith' in someone means to trust them.) They express terror rather than trust both before and after Jesus acts. Interestingly, just before this miracle, Jesus has told three parables whose point is that God's word is powerful. He then calms the storm with a word. The disciples should have drawn the obvious conclusion.

2. Books to read and recommend

Code: *Easy **Intermediate ***Advanced

Christian living

*Bridges, J., *Transforming Grace* (Colorado Springs: NavPress, 1991)
*Bridges, J., *Trusting God even when Life Hurts* (Colorado Springs: NavPress, 2001)
*Greene, M., *Thank God it's Monday* (London: Scripture Union, 2001)
*Roberts, V., *Distinctives* (Carlisle: Authentic Lifestyle, 2000)
**Carson, D., *How Long O Lord* (Leicester: IVP, 1990)
***Ryle, J.C., *Holiness* (Evangelical Press, 1979, 2001)

Evangelistic (to read and give away)

*Anderson, N., *The Evidence for the Resurrection* (Leicester: IVP, 2001)
*Chapman, J., *A Fresh Start* (London: Matthias Media, 1997)
*Dickson, J., *Stranger than Fiction* (London: Matthias Media)
*Roberts, V., *Turning Points* (Carlisle: Authentic Lifestyle, 1999)
*Tice, R., *Christianity Explored* (Carlisle: Authentic Lifestyle, 2002)
**Stott, J., *Basic Christianity* (Leicester: IVP, 1958)
**Strobel, L., *The Case for Christ* (Grand Rapids: Zondervan, 1998)

Evangelism

*Chapman, J., *Know and Tell the Gospel* (London: St Matthias Press, 1981)
**Packer, J.I., *Evangelism and the Sovereignty of God* (Leicester: IVP, 1961)

Prayer

*Dunn, R., *Don't Just Stand There, Pray Something* (Grand Rapids: Zondervan, 2001)
**Calvin, J., *Prayer* (London: Matthias Pocket Classics, 1997)
**Carson, D., *A Call to Spiritual Reformation* (Leicester: IVP, 1992)

Relationships and sex

*Harris, J., *Boy Meets Girl* (Sisters: Multnomah Publishers, 2000)
*Hsu, A., *The Single Issue* (Leicester: IVP, 1998)
*Keene, C., ed., *What Some of You Were* (on homosexuality) (London: Matthias Media, 2001)
*Pollock, N., *Relationships Revolution* (Leicester: IVP, 1998)
*Richardson, J., *God, Sex and Marriage* (London: Matthias Media,1995)
**Edwards, B., ed., *Homosexuality: the Straight Agenda* (Epsom: Day One, 1998)
**Jensen, P., *Pure Sex* (London: Matthias Media, 1998)

Biography

*Eareckson Tada, J., *The Joni Story* (London: Marshall Pickering, 1996)
*Elliot, E., *Through Gates of Splendour; Shadow of the Almighty; No Graven Image* (trilogy) (Carlisle: OM Publishing, 1997)
*Ten Boom, C., *The Hiding Place* (London: Hodder and Stoughton, 1971)
**Barclay, O., *From Cambridge to the World* (Leicester: IVP, 2002)
**Cormack, D., *Killing Fields, Living Fields* (Leicester: IVP, 1997)
**Pollock, J., *Hudson Taylor and Maria* (Tain: Christian Focus Publications, 1962)

**Ryle, J.C., *Five English Reformers* (Edinburgh: Banner of Truth, 1960)

Christian truth

*Meynell, M., *Cross Examined* (Leicester: IVP, 2001)
*Roberts, V., *True Worship* (Carlisle: Authentic Lifestyle, 2002)
**Packer, J.I., *Keep in Step with the Spirit* (Leicester: IVP, 1984)
**Packer, J.I., *Knowing God* (London: Hodder and Stoughton, 1973)
**Piper, J., *Desiring God* (Sisters: Multnomah Books, 1996)
***Carson, D., *The Difficult Doctrine of the Love of God* (Leicester: IVP, 2000)
***Milne, B., *Know the Truth* (Leicester: IVP, 1982)
***Stott, J., *The Cross of Christ* (Leicester: IVP, 1989)

The Bible

**Explore Bible Study Notes* (London: Good Book Company)
*Jensen and Payne, *Guidance and the Voice of God* (London: Matthias Media, 1997)
*Motyer, S., *The Bible with Pleasure* (Cambridge: Crossway Books, 1997)
*Richardson, J., *Get into the Bible* (London: St Matthias Press, 1994)
**Barnett, P., *Is the New Testament History?* (Carlisle: Paternoster Press, 1998)

**Goldsworthy, G., *Gospel and Kingdom* (Carlisle: Paternoster Press, 1991)
**Jackman, D., *I Believe in the Bible* (London: Hodder and Stoughton, 2000)
**Stott, J., *Understanding the Bible* (London: Scripture Union, 1972)
***Dumbrell, W., *The Faith of Israel* (Leicester: IVP, 2002)

Basic Bible commentaries

**Reading the Bible Today* series (London: Good Book Company)
***Bible Speaks Today* series (Leicester: IVP)
***Tyndale Commentaries* (Leicester: IVP)

3. Other helps

Tape ministry

Church audio ministries – e.g. St Helen's Church, Bishopsgate. email audio@shmedia.org.uk www.shmedia.org.uk; All Souls Church, Langham Place www.allsouls.org.uk;
Proclamation Trust Media www.proctrust.org.uk/home ptm.htm.
Good Book Company www.thegoodbook.co.uk.

Internet Resources

www.ccci.org/materials.html (Campus Crusade for Christ International) for Christian growth resources.

www.desiringgod.org for their Online Library.
www.gospelcom.net for different translations of the Bible (go to BibleGateway) and many other links.
www.thegoodbook.co.uk for Bible study resources, books, tapes, periodicals (all for purchase by order).
www.uccf.org.uk/cumovement/resources a number of very helpful articles on how to prepare and lead Bible studies, and several short Bible study series/courses.

Counselling organizations

Association of Christian Counsellors (ACC) – Head Office: 29 Momus Boulevard, Coventry, CV2 5NA Tel: 0845 124 9569/9570. Fax: 0845 124 9571. email office@acc-uk.org. Internet www.acc-uk.org.

This organization is a governing body for Christian counsellors who have a code of practice and accredit counsellors. If you contact the head office, they will refer you to your regional co-ordinator who can then put you in contact with an accredited counsellor.

Eating Disorders Association (EDA) –103 Prince of Wales Road, Norwich, NR1 1DW,United Kingdom.
Adult Helpline: 0845 634 1414 (open 8.30 to 20.30 weekdays).

Youthline: 0845 634 7650 (open 16.00 to 18.30 weekdays).
Admin: 0870 770 3256 (International No. +44 1603 619 090).
Media: 0870 770 3221 (International No. +44 1603 753316).
Fax: 0160 366 4915 (International No. +44 1603 664 915).
email: info@edauk.com. Internet www.edauk.com

Anorexia and Bulimia Care (ABC) – ABC, PO Box 30, Ormskirk, Lancs. L39 5ED, United Kingdom. Tel: +44 (0)1695 422 47. email doreen.abc@virgin.net. Internet www.anorexia bulimiacare.co.uk.

This is a Christian organization, which sufferers and their families may also wish to contact. Their mission statement is: 'We believe that there is an answer to anorexia, bulimia and compulsive eating and offer, from a Christian perspective, encouragement and support for the whole family to help make full recovery possible.'

True Freedom Trust – PO Box 13, Prenton, Wirral, CH43 6BY, United Kingdom. Tel: +44 (0)151 653 0773. Fax: +44 (0)151 653 7036. email to martin@tftrust.u-net.com. Internet: www.tftrust.u-net.com.

True Freedom Trust is a Christian support and teaching ministry offering hope and help to men and women struggling with homosexuality, lesbianism and similar issues. They also offer support to families, friends and church leaders of those who face these issues in their lives.

Church Pastoral Aid Society – Tel: +44 (0) 1926 458458; Internet: www.cpas.org.uk; email: info@cpas.org.uk.

The Churches' Child Protection Advisory Service – Tel; +44 (0) 845 120 4550; Internet: www.ccpas.org.uk; email: info@ccpas.org.uk.

Appendix
Growing your Relationship with God

The habit of daily setting aside time alone, usually in the morning, to feed from God's word and to pray has sustained Christians for centuries. In recent times it has often been referred to as a 'quiet time'.

Sadly, this time spent with God has sometimes been seen as a duty to be performed each day and then ticked off the 'to do' list – and when left unticked it has generated a lot of guilt and unnecessary angst. However, the fact that something that ought to be the fruit and fuel of a living relationship with our heavenly father can nonetheless be misconstrued and twisted by our sinful minds, is not to deny that it is a good thing to do! Where many of us struggle is in knowing exactly what we're supposed to be doing and how we can keep doing it with focus and sincerity without being distracted and feeling guilty all the time.

The typical quiet time consists of doing a small Bible study and then praying through a list. And yet, this attempt at communication with God can end up being so disjointed. We ask God to speak to us as we read his word, and he teaches us some amazing truths about who he is or what he's doing. We then shut our Bibles and speak back to him about quite unrelated things. There's something wrong with this kind of communication – the two parties don't seem to be relating meaningfully to each other. We're not really responding to what God is saying to us. When our devotional times are like this they can become a ritual and not a relationship.

Another problem with the traditional quiet time formula is what some have called 'spiritual indigestion'. We may be receiving so much spiritual food in the form of sermons, small group studies, one-to-one studies and then, on top of all that, our quiet time passages, that we are just overwhelmed by the intake and we don't digest any of it properly – it was never made real in our lives, it never really changes us. We can end up learning lots *about* God and his plans and yet still not get to know him any better.

How can we get beyond this? How can we hear God speaking to us in such a way that we take his word deep into our hearts and then respond to him, in genuine, loving dialogue?

Meditation

'Blessed is the man who ... delights in the law of the Lord, and on his law he meditates day and night' says the psalmist (Ps. 1:1–2). So how do we go about meditating on God's word? A good way to start is to take a truth from the Sunday sermon, or from your one-to-one prep, maybe, and mull it over, asking yourself questions to test your belief in and response to that truth. It means you're not having to necessarily 'work' at understanding a new passage every time – this is an opportunity rather to work through the application of a passage that you've already been taught or looked at yourself during the week (assuming that you are getting Bible input during the week). It's also a chance to take those truths and use them in our prayers – i.e. to respond to what God is actually saying to us.

Many of our spiritual problems in life stem from our failure to trust fully in God's word and his promises to us. If we really believed all that he says, we would surely live for him in a more radical way. In Mark 9, Jesus is talking to the father of a demon-possessed boy. This father has just asked Jesus to heal him saying, '"If you can do anything, take pity on us and help us." "If you can?" said Jesus. "Everything is possible for him who believes." Immediately the boy's father exclaimed, "I do believe; help me overcome my unbelief!" '

We too need God's help to overcome our unbelief and so enable us to trust and follow him. We need to wrestle truths through with God and work out their implications in our lives, praying for help to understand and to respond as we should – believing in his promises and finding our joy in knowing and serving him alone. Only he can truly satisfy.

When we meditate, we need to:

- Pray for understanding – and for God to really speak into our life.
- Take the message from the sermon, talk or study and check it again with the passage *or* get to that place ourselves by asking the right questions of a passage.
- Be clear on the main point/s and applications.
- Ask:

  a. Do I really believe this truth, or that God is serious in asking me to do this or that?

  b. In what ways do I show in my life that I don't really believe it or take what God is saying here seriously?

  c. Why don't I believe it? Why do I struggle with believing it so much?

d. How would my thinking and living change if I really took the point/application on board right now?

e. What is God's challenge for me today?

- Pray through the passage (see below), having mulled over the truth of that passage and thought through some of its implications.
- Give yourself time to meditate on the word 'day and night', keeping it on the front burner of our minds ourselves at times throughout the day.

Meditation is an ongoing process. You can use the same truth for days or even weeks if necessary. I once looked up all the possible Bible references to anxiety/worry and then all the characteristics of God that mean we don't need to worry, and mediated on them over a period of about two to three weeks. It is a very helpful way of absorbing God's word deep within ourselves so that we can preach to ourselves when we need to. Memorizing key verses or even whole passages can also be immensely helpful for the spiritual battle we face every day.

Meditation as the engine for our prayer life

It is once we have spent time wrestling with God's word and working through the implications for our life that we can then respond to God in prayer for ourselves and for others. Once we have heard from God and really listened to his word to us, we need to speak back to him about what he has said.

When we pray, it is often helpful to have some kind of structure as an aid to concentration, to keep us from being so easily distracted. I like to use the 'STOP' acronym:

Sorry – Confess known sins/unbelief/shortfalls/idolatry in the area you've been meditating on and pray for the Holy Spirit to reveal hidden areas of stubbornness and rebellion.

Thanks – Praise God for who he is (what you've learned from your meditation). Thank God for his forgiveness for your failings/unbelief, etc. Thank him for all he has done for you and blessed you with.

Others – Pray for friends, family, church, missionaries, Christians in other nations, for those in authority etc. in the light of the truth on which you've been meditating.

Please – Pray through the truth for your own life and specific situations that it might impact. Ask for help to believe God's word and for the power to respond to it. Ask for wisdom to make godly decisions, for comfort, for empowering, etc.

Many have found that spending time with God each day in this manner has led to a real growth in their relationship with God. There is a sense that you have really met with God as you have heard him speak, and have spent time wrestling through his word to you and responding to that word in confession, praise and intercession.

Endnotes

[1] Stott, J., *The Message of 2 Timothy* (The Bible Speaks Today) (Leicester: IVP, 1973), p.29. Published in North America by IVP, USA.

[2] Watson, D., *Discipleship* (London: Hodder and Stoughton, 1981), p.66. Reproduced by permission of Hodder and Stoughton Limited.

[3] Hendricks, H. and W., *As Iron Sharpens Iron* (Chicago, Il.: Moody Press, 1995), cover.

[4] Wookey, S., *When a Church Becomes a Cult* (London: Hodder and Stoughton, 1996), p.42. Reproduced by permission of Hodder and Stoughton Limited.

[5] Fryling, A., *The Disciplemakers' Handbook* (Leicester: IVP, 1989), p.65.

[6] Tice, R, *Christianity Explored Study Guide – Leader's Edition* (Carlisle: Authentic Lifestyle, 2003), selected studies